COUNCIL *on* **FOREIGN RELATIONS**

COUNCIL SPECIAL REPORT NO. 100

America Revived: A Grand Strategy of Resolute Global Leadership

By Robert D. Blackwill

January 2026

CONTENTS

FOREWORD

Much ink has been spilled lamenting the unprecedented foreign policy challenges, both internal and external, now confronting the United States: the rise of China, the return of great-power rivalry, the broad erosion of liberal internationalist assumptions and norms, and a growing domestic skepticism for the international obligations that defined the postwar order. In this timely Council Special Report, the Council's Henry A. Kissinger senior fellow for U.S. foreign policy, Robert D. Blackwill, makes clear that the era of admiring these problems is over. Instead, Blackwill proposes a revised American grand strategy to meet the present moment of global dislocation head-on.

Blackwill's central achievement, beyond proposing a new design, is to reconcile the competing, historical doctrines of American grand strategy with the contemporary challenges the United States now faces, while situating those debates within both the current political environment and the country's long, often uneasy, relationship with the mantle of global leadership. He treats the major schools of American grand strategy—primacy, liberal internationalism, restraint, American nationalism, and Trumpism—with intellectual fairness, laying bare not only what each promises but what each exacts in cost and risk. The result is a reminder that grand strategy is not a moral posture but a series of hard choices subject to constraints, and that, as Blackwill writes, there is no strategy without trade-offs.

Blackwill's proposal arrives at a moment when many Americans question whether the burdens of leadership are worth bearing. Alliances have been recast as liabilities, global trade as a zero-sum bilateral contest, and global governance institutions as naïve indulgences. In such a climate, the temptation is to confuse retrenchment with restraint, transactionalism with durable statecraft, and, most dangerously, to mistake the end of the unipolar moment and waning enthusiasm for liberal internationalism for the need to recast American national interests from whole cloth. Yet, as this report makes clear, "abdicating the United States' global military presence" is not a benign experiment. Followed to its logical conclusion, Blackwill argues, the ascendant schools of restraint and Trumpism rest on assumptions that are "dangerous to test," premised on the hope that U.S. withdrawal would enhance both prosperity and security, a claim that remains uncorroborated and fraught with risk. A free and open Indo-Pacific is not self-sustaining, nor is a world shaped by Chinese economic and technological dominance an inevitable end state. More to the point, it is much easier to lose one's perch than to regain it, particularly when faced with a competitor of China's size and skill.

We have, of course, been here before, albeit with our eyes focused on the European theater. As Blackwill reminds us, the concept of grand strategy crystallized during the interwar period, when thinkers such as Liddell Hart, Corbett, Fuller, and Earle grappled with how modern states marshal all instruments of national power amid technological upheaval, economic interdependence, and systemic instability. Then, as now, the United States faced a choice between withdrawal or sustained leadership in shaping the international system. In the end, strategic success depended less on consensus than on clarity and on a willingness to resist, or at least temper, the political fashions of the moment.

Blackwill's latest contribution to this tradition of American strategic thought is a sixth school: resolute global leadership. Anchored in the logic of "peace through strength," it accepts China as a peer competitor, rejects fantasies of costless dominance and costless disengagement, and insists that American leadership—military, economic, and institutional—remains the least bad option in what might otherwise slip into a fully Hobbesian world. It combines the hard-power emphasis of primacy with the alliance-centered and institutional insights of liberal internationalism, emphasizing U.S. military superiority while also leveraging allies, partners, and international systems as force multipliers rather than substitutes for power.

The question Blackwill ultimately leaves us with is therefore the right one. Will the United States rediscover, through civil discourse and choice, the virtues of leadership and internationalism that underpinned its postwar success, or, as in 1941, will it require a great cataclysm to rehabilitate them? For now, we retain the luxury of contemplation—informed by this fine report.

Michael Froman
President
Council on Foreign Relations
January 2026

ACKNOWLEDGMENTS

I am grateful for the thoughtful comments of Council on Foreign Relations President Mike Froman, who first suggested this project, Director of Studies Shannon O'Neil, and Associate Vice President of Studies Stuart Reid. For their insights over eight sessions from October 2024 to May 2025, I am indebted to the sixty members of the CFR Study Group on Alternative U.S. Grand Strategies. This Council Special Report benefited from the presentations to the study group by Eric Edelman, Peter Feaver, Richard Fontaine, Ionut Popescu, Barry Posen, Anne-Marie Slaughter, Stephen Wertheim, and Robert Zoellick. I am also appreciative of critiques of the text by Graham Allison, Richard Haass, Sean Mirski, Ashley Tellis, Philip Zelikow, and Robert Zoellick.

Special thanks to Turner Ruggi for his invaluable research and logistical management; to Kendall Carll, Alex Gerstenhaber, and Lee Block for their research assistance; and to Patricia Dorff and Cassandra Jensen for their editorial contributions.

I alone am responsible for the analysis and conclusions presented here.

Robert D. Blackwill

EXECUTIVE SUMMARY

The United States faces the most dangerous international circumstances since the end of World War II, and perhaps in its history. An ever more formidable, authoritarian China remains determined to replace the United States as the leading nation in Asia and eventually the world. The need for an effective U.S. grand strategy to deal with that threat, among others, is accordingly urgent. Grand strategy refers to a nation's collective deployment of all its relevant instruments of power to accomplish key strategic goals. Given the United States' longtime material, institutional, and ideational strengths, American grand strategy involves projecting its great power for the survival of world order. To that end, sustaining prosperity, which derives substantially from the United States' dominance in technological innovation, becomes the economic precondition for protecting its own homeland, the homelands of its allies, and its diverse national interests. It can achieve those goals through both military and non-military methods, but force is acceptable only if it represents an inescapable choice to protect vital national interests. Promoting democracy is never such an inescapable choice.

This report analyzes five alternative schools of American grand strategy and then proposes a sixth school, resolute global leadership. The primacy school of grand strategy, which includes neoconservatism, asserts that the United States must remain the world's unrivaled superpower in every region and, toward that end, prevent the reemergence of a peer competitor. The liberal internationalist school envisions a U.S.-led, open, rules-based world order that champions the rule of law, liberal democracy, and human rights, and accepts using military force as a last resort to safeguard U.S. vital national interests. The restraint school, often associated with realism and offshore balancing and scarred by recent unsuccessful wars, seeks to slash American global commitments and argues that U.S. military intervention is almost always ill-advised. The American nationalist school insists that the United States should concentrate its attention and strength on the Western Hemisphere, that previous presidents have foolishly agreed to trade and security agreements that hollowed out the nation's economy, and that only U.S. power, not alliances and global organizations, guarantees enduring benefits for the United States. And Trumpism, a version of American nationalism that depends on the personal preferences of President Donald Trump, radically redefines U.S. vital national interests to emphasize bilateral and transactional trade relationships, business deals, and quick diplomatic successes over geopolitical considerations—without collaboration with traditional U.S. allies or fidelity to core American values, including human rights.

This report argues that the competing strategies of restraint, American nationalism, and Trumpism all fail on different counts. Restraint presumes that abdicating the United States' global military presence will enhance both prosperity and security, a claim that has not yet been corroborated and is dangerous to test. American nationalism discounts international legitimacy and complaisantly expects that the United States can uphold prosperity and security by focusing predominantly, if not exclusively, on the U.S. homeland and its hemisphere and on bilateral trade. And Trumpism risks undermining the nation's prosperity, security, and legitimacy simultaneously because of its determination to advance American national interests at the expense of others.

Drawing from the grand strategies of primacy and liberal internationalism, the grand strategy of resolute global leadership is superior to all other alternatives. Like primacy, it affirms the importance of American military might, especially potent instruments for deterrence and force projection, to parry varied threats and defend the United States and its allies as far forward as possible to preserve favorable balances of power in critical regions. But unlike primacy, resolute global leadership accepts that China has emerged as a peer competitor, and this grand strategy does not believe in using military force for ideological goals. Like liberal internationalism, resolute global leadership emphasizes the requirement to underwrite international institutions, both to increase U.S. and worldwide prosperity and to create an international environment conducive to U.S. national interests. Resolute global leadership recognizes, however, that military power is still central to geopolitics, and it treats global institutions as important but useful only insofar as they advance those interests.

Although the current political landscape is unfavorable to resolute global leadership, it is the best grand strategy to sustain prosperity, enhance security, and cement the legitimacy of the United States as a powerful force in the international system. When the country confronts the implications of its experiment with Trumpism, resolute global leadership will offer the clearest route to a revival of American strength.

INTRODUCTION

The United States faces the most dangerous international circumstances since the end of World War II, and perhaps in its history.[1] An ever more powerful authoritarian China plows ahead in its determined effort to replace the United States as the dominant power in the Indo-Pacific, and eventually the world.[2] As former Singaporean Prime Minister Lee Kuan Yew, a lifelong advocate of U.S. power projection into Asia, drilled home, "[t]he U.S. cannot stop China's rise. It just has to live with a bigger China, which will be completely novel for the U.S., as no country has ever been big enough to challenge its position. . . . It is not possible to pretend that this is just another big player. This is the biggest player in the history of the world."[3]

To confront the China challenge, address other threats to U.S. national interests, and seize opportunities when they arise, the United States requires an effective grand strategy. That demands sustained coordination of U.S. foreign policy in the face of limited resources.

This Council Special Report defines grand strategy, analyzes its fundamental connection to American vital national interests, surveys grand strategies the United States has followed since 1776, tests the strengths and weaknesses of five alternative U.S. grand strategies for the next decade and beyond (primacy, liberal internationalism, restraint, American nationalism, and Trumpism), and proposes a composite U.S. grand strategy of resolute global leadership for this dynamic era.

Although the term "grand strategy" can be traced back to at least the nineteenth century, the modern formulation originated in the works of military scholars B. H. Liddell Hart, J. F. C. Fuller, Julian S. Corbett, and Edward M. Earle during the interwar period.[4] For Liddell Hart, "the role of grand strategy—higher strategy—is to coordinate and direct all the resources of a nation, or band of nations, toward the attainment of the political object of the war."[5] Likewise, Fuller argued that grand strategy was the synchronization of "all war-like resources towards the winning of the war."[6] Thus, the main tenet of grand strategy emerged: the collective deployment of diplomatic, economic, military, ideological, moral, and bureaucratic means to attain strategic ends.[7] That expansion of the idea inevitably led to the recognition that grand strategy pertains to a larger realm beyond conflict. As captured succinctly by international relations scholar Joshua Rovner, while strategy simply describes a "theory of victory"—"how to use force in order to achieve political objectives in war"—grand strategy represents "a theory of security," that is, "how to make oneself safe in an unsafe world."[8]

The primacy school of grand strategy, including neoconservatism, asserts that the United States must remain the world's unrivaled superpower and, toward that end, prevent the reemergence of a peer competitor.[9] The liberal internationalist school envisions an open, U.S.-led, rules-based world order that champions the rule of law, liberal democracy, and human rights, and accepts using military force as a last resort to safeguard U.S. vital national interests. There are critical differences between primacy and liberal internationalism, as the former prefers more often to use military force—including escalatory measures—on behalf of vital national interests, while the latter employs it only as a last resort and otherwise wishes to build a rules-based world order led by the United States through international organizations.

The restraint school, often associated with realism and offshore balancing and scarred by unsuccessful recent wars, seeks to slash American global commitments and argues that U.S. military intervention is almost always ill-advised.[10] The American nationalist school insists that the United States should concentrate its attention and strength on the Western Hemisphere, that previous presidents have foolishly agreed to trade and security agreements that hollowed out the nation's economy, and that only U.S. power, not alliances and global organizations, guarantees enduring benefits for the United States. And Trumpism, a particular version of American nationalism that depends on the personal preferences of President Donald Trump, radically redefines U.S. vital national interests to emphasize bilateral and transactional trade relationships, business deals, and quick diplomatic successes over geopolitical considerations—without collaboration with traditional U.S. allies or fidelity to core American values, including human rights. Those three schools question U.S. international commitments, but for vastly different reasons: restraint seeks to prevent the United States from getting dragged into a conflict that does not directly affect vital interests; American nationalism preoccupies itself with the Western Hemisphere and restoring domestic industry; and Trumpism, while endorsing many elements of American nationalism—including a "Trump Corollary" to the Monroe Doctrine—pursues global diplomatic and commercial successes.

Given the wide diversity of opinion within each school, however, those thumbnail sketches of alternative grand strategies should not obscure that this subject is a notoriously slippery concept for scholars and policymakers alike. Moreover, American presidents sometimes stray from the purest principles of the grand strategy that they profess. As former U.S. Secretary of State Henry Kissinger noted, "No country can act wisely simultaneously in every part of the globe at every moment in time."[11] And statesman and U.S. Army General George Marshall emphasized that, when deciding what to do, one is also deciding what not to do, a difficult task for every government at every level.[12] Thus, grand strategy requires clear national objectives that the strategy aims to achieve, best framed through an articulation of U.S. national interests.

Since President George Washington's farewell address, core U.S. national interests have not changed: to ensure the fundamental security of the homeland and its people. As another founding father, Alexander Hamilton, phrased it, "Self preservation is the first duty of a Nation."[13] And until the resurgence of American nationalism and the advent of Trumpism in the past decade, U.S. vital national interests for seventy years after World War II were defined by a bipartisan consensus, with more recent revisions that reflect new threats:

- to prevent the use and reduce the threat of nuclear, biological, and chemical weapons and to ward off conventional attacks as well as catastrophic terrorist assaults or cyberattacks against the United States, its military forces abroad, or its allies;

- to stop the spread of nuclear weapons, secure nuclear weapons and materials, and reduce further proliferation of delivery systems for nuclear weapons;

- to prevent the emergence of hostile major powers or failed states in the Western Hemisphere;

- to maintain global and regional balances of power, especially in Eurasia, that promote peace, stability, and freedom through domestic U.S. strength, the projection of U.S. power and influence abroad, and the vitality of U.S. alliances; and

- to ensure the viability and stability of major international systems (trade, financial markets, public health, energy supplies, cyberspace, the environment, freedom of the seas, and outer space).[14]

Today, China challenges all five of those vital U.S. national interests.[15]

The most elegant and refined grand strategy is not a detailed road map to future success, but at best only a conceptual compass inevitably filled with uncertainties. As British historian Frederic William Maitland is credited with saying, "one must remember that events long in the past were once in the future." Despite what is sometimes taught in academia, grand strategy is not complete when discussed in the abstract, untouched by implementation, the responses of other actors, erroneous and incomplete information, insufficient analysis, errors in judgment, bureaucratic and personality conflicts, and all the other inherent weaknesses of the human species. Unsurprisingly, therefore, successful U.S. grand strategy hinges on the quality of the people who develop and implement it, beginning with the president.

The United States should not despair. It possesses enormous strength and capacity to sculpt world order, even if that power is often underused or misapplied. Although the current political landscape is unfavorable to resolute global leadership, it is the best grand strategy to sustain prosperity, enhance security, and cement the legitimacy of the United States as a powerful force in the international system. When the country confronts the implications of the Trumpism experiment, resolute global leadership will offer the clearest route to a revival of American strength.

THE HISTORY OF
U.S. GRAND STRATEGY

The American Revolution marked the start of U.S. grand strategy, as the colonies marshaled military, economic, and diplomatic means to achieve a single goal: independence.[16] Diplomacy was indispensable as the 1778 alliance with France secured vital financial and security assistance and ultimately culminated in the 1783 Treaty of Paris, which affirmed the United States as an independent nation.[17] From there, the consolidation of the young republic and noninterference from colonial powers crystallized as the United States' primary strategic objectives. To steer the new nation away from entanglement in European conflicts, Washington first issued the 1793 Proclamation of Neutrality and subsequently endorsed a broader policy of neutrality in his farewell address.[18]

By the turn of the nineteenth century, the new nation had pivoted to a century-long grand strategy of American nationalism.[19] It sought to conquer and fortify the continental homeland, shore up regional security under the banner of the 1823 Monroe Doctrine, steer clear of Europe, and expand international trade and investment—especially in China, Japan, Korea, the Philippines, and Latin America—through favorable balances of power to the United States' commercial advantage.[20] In the early twentieth century, President Theodore Roosevelt, following the war between the United States and Spain that ended Spanish colonial rule in the Americas and resulted in U.S. acquisition of territories in the western Pacific and Latin America, launched a flurry of diplomatic activity in the Western Hemisphere and Asia, including negotiating the end of the Russo–Japanese conflict.

Once the old empires became mired in the trenches of World War I, however, the United States' long-standing avoidance of European involvement briefly gave way for the first time to a grand strategy of liberal internationalism, as outlined in President Woodrow Wilson's Fourteen Points. Wilson aimed to build a stable, rules-based international system through multilateral cooperation enshrined in the League of Nations and the projection of American values to render the world "safe for democracy."[21] But those historically radical objectives stirred up a domestic political hornet's nest, and Wilson failed to carry either the Senate or the country.

Beginning with the Coolidge administration in 1923, U.S. grand strategy again championed American nationalism, including a concentration on the Western Hemisphere and a continuation of high tariffs.[22]

As Nazi Germany surged in the 1930s, President Franklin D. Roosevelt maneuvered against strong domestic public opinion to attempt to slowly rewire U.S. grand strategy from American nationalism to liberal internationalism, with its emphasis on avoiding a hegemon on the Eurasian landmass.[23] Whether he would otherwise have succeeded domestically in enshrining liberal internationalism became moot when, in December 1941, Japan attacked Pearl Harbor and German Chancellor Adolf Hitler declared war on the United States.[24]

As the Soviet Union's aggressive intentions became clear in the years following World War II and were propelled by the Korean War in June 1950, liberal internationalism became the enduring U.S. grand strategy.[25] It was anchored in the belief that only American global leadership could prevent a hostile hegemon, in this case the Soviet Union, from overrunning Eurasia and destabilizing world order. Liberal internationalism's principles were reflected in U.S. diplomat George F. Kennan's "Long Telegram," which advocated containment of the USSR; the Truman Doctrine; the Marshall Plan; the Berlin Airlift; the creation of NATO; and the National Security Council report NSC-68—all of which embodied U.S. power and democratic values to forge and safeguard a stable international system.[26] Not surprisingly, those developments were anathema to the American nationalists, who were beginning many decades in the U.S. policy desert.[27]

A liberal internationalist, President Lyndon Johnson committed over five hundred thousand troops to Vietnam by believing that the hegemonic objectives of China and the Soviet Union had, in part, generated North Vietnam's intervention in South Vietnam. In that context, the restraint school was born, arguing for a dramatically scaled-back global military footprint, emphasizing the need to eviscerate overseas commitments, and stressing that U.S. military intervention almost always compromised U.S. security.[28] The restraint grand strategy, however, although popular to this day in some political and academic quarters, failed to gain traction as American government policy.[29]

President Richard Nixon and Kissinger maintained most of the liberal internationalist principles of Presidents Harry S. Truman, Dwight D. Eisenhower, John F. Kennedy, and Johnson but made great power diplomacy paramount through the opening to China and détente with the USSR.[30] Presidents Gerald Ford and Jimmy Carter sustained those

Nixonian initiatives, although Carter also accentuated core American values in U.S. grand strategy, such as the protection of human rights.[31] As détente eventually unraveled through Soviet adventurism, U.S. grand strategy shifted to a more confrontational form of liberal internationalism under President Ronald Reagan, with major increases in defense spending to combat the Soviet Union.

After the collapse of the USSR during the classically liberal internationalist George H.W. Bush presidency, a grand strategy of primacy was possible for the first time in U.S. history.[32] In that unipolar period, liberal internationalist Presidents Bill Clinton and George W. Bush could have piloted a primacist grand strategy but did not do so. Bush's campaigns in Afghanistan and Iraq laid bare that even with its enormous power, the United States could not force success in those regional conflicts.

By the mid-2010s, as the rise of Chinese power gradually dissolved the possibility of American primacy, President Barack Obama worked to sustain a liberal internationalist order, including through the Paris climate accord, the Iran nuclear agreement, the New START Treaty, and the ill-fated Trans-Pacific Partnership (TPP).[33] Condemning liberal internationalism, Trump in his first term illustrated his American nationalist impulses even as his conservative national security advisors partially hemmed him in. He exited the Iran nuclear agreement, the Paris climate accord, and the World Health Organization; withdrew from the Intermediate-Range Nuclear Forces and Open Skies Treaties with Russia; continuously disparaged the U.S. alliance system; and started a trade war with China.[34] Then, in 2020, lifetime liberal internationalist Joe Biden was elected president. In office, he invested in U.S. alliances and rejoined international agreements.[35]

On his return to the White House in 2025, Trump, no longer checked by establishment advisors, unleashed a radical departure in American foreign policy that repudiated the post–World War II consensus on U.S. vital national interests and centered American power and prestige almost solely on the occupant of the Oval Office. Given past policy and current power realities, Trump's potential successor will have six grand strategies from which to choose.

PRIMACY

Pillars of Primacy

The nine pillars of primacy are as follows:

- Promote American global and regional military, economic, and diplomatic hegemony by preventing the rise of any peer competitor, substantially expanding the defense budget, employing military force—including escalatory measures—on behalf of vital U.S. interests, undertaking nation-building when necessary, and ensuring victory in the high-technology race with China.

- Maintain a rules-based international order through overriding American dominance.

- Prevent the use and spread of nuclear weapons.

- Pivot U.S. security forces to Asia to prevent China's hegemonic objectives, drawing down U.S. military deployments in Europe and the Middle East while maintaining regional leadership, security commitments, and a presence in both theaters.

- Urge U.S. allies in both Asia and Europe to play a much greater role in regional security and deterrence, with substantially increased defense spending.

- Strengthen U.S. alliances and enhance bilateral partnerships through diplomacy, especially to deal with China, Iran, North Korea, Russia, and international terrorism.

- Use American unipolar power to preserve the viability and stability of major global systems and institutions for trade, financial markets, freedom of the seas, energy, space, and health.

- Bolster U.S. preeminence by using force to promote domestic democratic institutions and practices in selective situations.

- Favor market-based approaches to clean technology over binding international emissions targets as the preferred strategy for combating climate change.[36]

Defense of Primacy

For both its own national interests and the largely U.S.-engineered world order, primacy proclaims that the United States should abide as the world's sole superpower.[37] In the primacist view, the U.S. as the single global hegemon, unrivaled in its ability to project diplomatic, military, and economic power, furnishes the public goods essential to world peace and prosperity.

Primacists believe that the United States should block threats not only to American national interests but also to the interests of Washington's allies and partners.[38] Enforcing a U.S. alliance system dissuades nations from conflict with each other and deters potential adversaries.[39] No lesser coalition of like-minded middle powers can muster the necessary military force and political will to deal with predatory international aggressors and shepherd world order. Without sustained American hegemonic power and leadership, conflict among contending major powers is potentially only a crisis away. "The alternative to Pax Americana—the *only* alternative—is global disorder," columnist Bret Stephens opined in 2014.[40]

Preponderant American might is the cornerstone of primacist grand strategy. Only dominant U.S. military power provides the basis for effective deterrence; diplomacy regarding China, Russia, aggressive rogue states, terrorism, and proliferation; and the promotion of democracy through force. It underpins and assures the stability of American global leadership and world order. As former Secretary of State George Shultz stressed, "Strength, strength, strength. Never let it leave your mind."[41]

Critique of Primacy

Critics of primacy argue that it was constructed during a brief twenty-year bygone era, as extinct as VCRs. Conceived in a transitory unipolar moment, it misreads a current world in which power is widely diffused and a peer competitor—China—increasingly challenges U.S. regional and global dominance.[42] Primacy breeds global dynamics that compel Washington to contend with ever more problems with limited resources, too much ambition, and too little regional knowledge. American preeminence encourages partners to free ride on the U.S. taxpayer and to act recklessly because they are confident of rock-hard American assistance.[43] Primacy's weaknesses echo Senator J. William Fulbright's 1966 assertion that "power confuses itself with virtue and tends also to take itself for omnipotence."[44]

LIBERAL INTERNATIONALISM

Pillars of Liberal Internationalism

The nine pillars of liberal internationalism are as follows:

- Foster via diplomacy a rules-based world order led by the United States through international organizations, democratic coalitions, and like-minded partners.

- Prevent the use or spread of nuclear weapons through diplomacy and, if necessary, force.

- Maintain deterrence and a stable global and regional balance of power through diplomacy, without increases in the defense budget or major U.S. military interventions.

- Manage China's expansionist international objectives as a peer competitor using active diplomacy, while avoiding U.S.-China military conflict through strong alliances, U.S. soft power, American values, and global opinion—and collaborate with China to promote international institutional reform and regulation, including with respect to high technologies.

- Urge U.S. allies in both Asia and Europe to play a much greater role in regional security and deterrence, with substantially increased defense spending.

- Strengthen U.S. alliances and enhance bilateral partnerships through diplomacy, especially to deal with China, Iran, North Korea, Russia, international terrorism, and global challenges.

- Advance the viability and stability of major global systems and institutions for trade, financial markets, freedom of the seas, energy, space, and health.

- Support vigorously democracy and human rights around the world, and consider using military force to avert genocide.

- Address climate change as a profound global threat requiring multilateral cooperation, binding international agreements, and U.S. leadership in environmental standards.[45]

Defense of Liberal Internationalism

Liberal internationalism seeks a world order based on international law, intense diplomacy, multilateral institutions, and the global spread of democracy, human rights, and prosperity while avoiding using major U.S. military force.[46] According to this school, the international system should be upheld by collective institutions such as NATO, the United Nations, the World Bank, the International Monetary Fund, and the World Trade Organization, as well as ad hoc coalitions of like-minded states, with the promotion of democracy as a central guiding principle. Liberal internationalism facilitated democratic transitions and economic liberalization globally. It created a framework for post–World War II economic rebuilding and fostered alliances where former enemies became partners. It established a decades-long deterrence and defense strategy that avoided war among major powers. There are not sufficient reasons to abandon this extraordinarily successful grand strategy.[47] As Kennedy insisted in 1960, "peace must be based on world law and world order, on the mutual respect of all nations for the rights and powers of others."[48]

Even if American relative power and influence wane, liberal internationalists assert that their grand strategy can survive.[49] That is because if the rules-based international order is stewarded through a partnership of nations large and small, rather than through balance-of-power rivalries, then the system's stability will endure even if one state's influence diminishes.[50]

Unlike proponents of the other schools of grand strategy, liberal internationalists also call for greater U.S. engagement with nonstate actors such as civil-society groups, nongovernmental organizations, social media platforms, multinational businesses, and even private individuals. As New America CEO Anne-Marie Slaughter argues, "without these stakeholders, the world does not have the resources, reach, expertise, or energy necessary to achieve the agendas it has set for itself."[51]

Critique of Liberal Internationalism

Critics charge that liberal internationalism rests on wishful thinking about both the conduct of nation-states and the character of humanity. They point out that in the past fifteen years, liberal internationalism has failed to halt China's militarization of the South China Sea and resist its mounting pressure on Taiwan; to punish Russian aggression in Crimea and the Donbas, which emboldened Moscow's full-scale invasion of Ukraine in 2022; to quickly send the most advanced weapons to Ukraine to defend itself; to halt Iran's proxies, which grew in strength and capability across the Middle East; to permanently prevent Iran's enrichment of uranium well beyond the 3 percent threshold for civilian use; to enforce its "red line" on Syria's chemical weapons use; to avoid an unwise and disastrous withdrawal of U.S. troops from Afghanistan with severe damage to American credibility and competence; to defend the international trading system that brought untold global prosperity; and to safeguard the U.S. southern border.[52]

Moreover, according to critics, many countries essential to advancing U.S. national interests fail to meet the democratic standards of liberal internationalism—including Brazil, Egypt, Indonesia, Pakistan, Turkey, Vietnam, and the Gulf monarchies. That traps liberal internationalist governments in a permanent bind—either adhere to their core democratic principles and thus compromise American national interests or shelve those principles to protect the nation.

Finally, some liberal internationalists are what could be called multipolar pessimists.[53] In their worldview, the fundamentals of world order have permanently shifted, and American power has so thinned that the United States can no longer decisively shape the international system. That means that in this new world, the United States needs to reexamine every principle of liberal internationalism, since none now has prima facie virtue.[54]

Their critics argue, however, that those strategists chronically underestimate the American capacity to decisively mold world order. The United States commands roughly the same share (26 percent) of global gross domestic product (GDP) as it held in the early 1990s.[55] It fields the world's most powerful military, devoting $849 billion to defense in 2025.[56] It possesses global diplomatic reach, if deftly exercised. Its treaty alliances and close partnerships in Asia, Europe, and the Middle East remain intact. And its power outmatches all the emerging nations combined, which in any case harbor sharply differing views on many global issues.[57]

RESTRAINT

Pillars of Restraint

The nine pillars of restraint are as follows:

- Recognize that global politics has no central authority and that states are forced to defend themselves, as international cooperation is fragile.

- Reduce radically U.S. global forward military deployments and security commitments, and do not wage unnecessary wars because few foreign policy crises threaten U.S. vital national interests.

- Enhance democracy and human rights through diplomacy, never through force and never through ideological nation-building.

- Shrink substantially the U.S. defense budget.

- Demand that U.S. allies in both Asia and Europe play the primary role in regional security and deterrence.

- Prevent the use or spread of nuclear weapons through diplomacy.

- Manage China's regional and global objectives through intense U.S.-China diplomacy and strong American alliances, while collaborating with China to promote international reform and stability, including with respect to high technologies.

- Advance the viability and stability of major global systems and institutions for trade, financial markets, freedom of the seas, energy, space, and health.

- Engage in vigorous international cooperation to address climate change.[58]

Defense of Restraint

Proponents of restraint echo Secretary of State John Quincy Adams in 1821: "Wherever the standard of freedom and Independence, has been or shall be unfurled, there will her heart, her benedictions and her prayers be. But she goes not abroad, in search of monsters to destroy. She is the well-wisher to the freedom and independence of all. She is the champion and vindicator only of her own."[59]

Deeply scarred by what it regards as failed wars, including those in Afghanistan, Iraq, Korea, and Vietnam, the restraint school argues that U.S. military interventions consistently weaken the nation.[60] However good the intentions, using force inevitably makes bad situations worse through U.S. overreach, arrogance, ignorance, deeply flawed policies, unintended consequences, and eventual loss of public support. Thus, diplomacy should in almost every case be the sole instrument to protect and promote U.S. vital national interests.

Promising to dramatically cut costs and risks, a grand strategy of restraint aims to reduce American global commitments, lower the defense budget, shrink U.S. force structure, bring home most U.S. military deployments abroad, and reject using military force unless there is an immediate threat to the homeland. In that context, U.S. allies and friends should shoulder responsibility for their regions' security, with the United States providing diplomatic support and, if hostile hegemonic objectives arise such as in Ukraine, with it supplying financial aid and military equipment too.

In short, if the United States continues to search abroad for dragons to slay, it will continue to find them at the nation's expense.

Critique of Restraint

According to critics, it is delusional to suggest that the United States can safeguard its national interests and preserve world order by substantially diminishing its international power and influence, markedly pruning its global security commitments, dismantling its extensive network of U.S. foreign bases, and assuming U.S. allies and friends will effectively fall in behind.[61] American withdrawal would spawn security vacuums in every vital region, which adversaries (such as China, Iran, North Korea, and Russia) would exploit. Because prospects for resistance without U.S. support would dim, allies and partners would grow ever more vulnerable to hostile pressure, while the United States itself would lose the ability to prevent regional hegemons from dominating areas vital to its economic and security interests.[62]

Strategist Frank Hoffman underlined the point in 2016: "Were we living in the 1990s, at the apex of the Unipolar Era, this strategy [restraint] would be relevant. Today, it risks power vacuums, entices regional aggression, and puts U.S. military forces at both a strategic and operational disadvantage."[63]

Finally, critics allege that there is no reason to believe that the planet's other major challenges—climate, sanctity of sovereign borders, the global economy, pandemics, international terrorism, and mass migration—can be effectively addressed without decisive American global involvement and leadership. "The price of greatness is responsibility," British Prime Minister Winston Churchill admonished in a 1943 speech. "One cannot rise to be in many ways the leading community in the civilized world without being involved in its problems, without being convulsed by its agonies and inspired by its causes."[64]

AMERICAN NATIONALISM

Pillars of American Nationalism

The nine pillars of American nationalism are as follows:

- Reject the classic post–World War II expression of U.S. vital national interests.

- Abandon multilateral diplomacy as an instrument to promote U.S. national interests.

- Ensure that any use or spread of nuclear weapons does not endanger the American people.

- Use U.S. military force only to neutralize direct threats in the Western Hemisphere.

- Flatline or lower U.S. defense spending.

- Declare that the United States should not defend treaty allies in Asia or Europe.

- Pursue protectionist trade policies to maximize the U.S. trade surplus, win the high-technology race (including artificial intelligence [AI]), and bring American companies back to the United States.

- Refuse to interfere in the domestic affairs of other nations, including to defend human rights.

- Dismiss climate concerns, partly because of constraints on U.S. sovereignty.[65]

Defense of American Nationalism

For almost the entire post–World War II period, the Washington elite took for granted that American leadership to advance a stable and interconnected world order best served U.S. national interests. American nationalists reject that view and the historic bipartisan consensus on U.S. vital national interests.

They seek to reclaim a bygone era—before the United States underwrote, indeed largely created, the world order after World War II. At its core, that grand strategy prescribes limited global engagement and champions a foreign policy that cements American dominance in the Western Hemisphere and locks in advantageous access to foreign markets. It asserts that since 1945, U.S. allies have taken advantage of American power, global institutions have handcuffed the United States, and foreign crises have dragged the country into a string of failed wars.[66]

Global trade is a central foreign policy concern for American nationalists. They charge that globalization, incompetent U.S. negotiators, and unfair trade agreements have prevented prosperity for U.S. workers over the decades. To ensure a healthy economy in which middle-class Americans flourish, only protectionist trade policies, tariffs, and a positive balance of payments will deliver the goods.[67]

Finally, American nationalists dismiss threats to U.S. vital national interests from China (except as they menace the U.S. economy); the outcome of the war in Ukraine; Iran's quest for a nuclear weapon; or the plight of billions in the developing world.[68] They believe that those dangers do not touch the prosperity and quality of life of the American worker and certainly do not justify using U.S. military force, which should be confined to the Western Hemisphere, including against illegal migration across the U.S. southern border.[69]

U.S. statesman Henry Cabot Lodge in 1919 expressed the essence of American nationalism: "The United States is the world's best hope, but if you fetter her in the interests and quarrels of other nations . . . you will destroy her power for good and endanger her very existence."[70]

Critique of American Nationalism

Opponents of American nationalism point out that the U.S.-steered post–World War II world order served as the basis for the most extraordinary advances ever in the human condition, including in the United States, and brought safety and prosperity to billions around the globe.[71] It averted war among the great powers for the longest period in five centuries and prevented the use and slowed the spread of nuclear weapons.[72] It is that enormously beneficial world order that American nationalists aim to deconstruct.

Critics argue that by scorning diplomacy and alliances, American nationalism abandons a crucial U.S. advantage against China: the United States' network of collaborative democratic allies and regional partners with shared national interests. If Washington does not contest Chinese hostile actions in the Indo-Pacific and beyond, Beijing would eventually squeeze the Western Hemisphere and U.S. regional and global trade, at which point the United States would be compelled to respond from a weakened position. It would blunt the U.S. ability to capitalize on some of the largest and fastest-growing global economies. It would deny Washington access to critical resources required for emerging high technologies. It would embolden Russia to further territorial aggression in Europe, which would again pull the United States into war through the NATO Article 5 commitment or, worse, leave it to watch as hegemonic powers subjugate Eurasia. It would disrupt the Middle East, risk terrorist attacks on the American homeland, and destabilize world energy prices.

Further, opponents assert that American nationalist protectionist tariffs would hobble the U.S. economy based on the false premise that the United States can resurrect the industrial economy of the 1950s.[73] Though framed as tools to dominate high-tech industries such as AI or to reduce the trade deficit, those measures would sap U.S. innovation, investment, and supply chain efficiencies that spring from global economic integration, and over time would erode the quality of life of American workers.[74]

In short, critics believe that American nationalism would leave the United States poorer, weaker, and more vulnerable to the very dangers it seeks to avoid.

TRUMPISM

Pillars of Trumpism

The nine pillars of Trumpism are as follows:

- Question the classic post–World War II expression of U.S. vital national interests, while pursuing Trump's personalized foreign policies and practices.[75]

- Regard bilateral trade, not geopolitics, as the driving engine of vital American national interests, which previous presidents have systematically undermined.[76]

- Assert that the overriding U.S. security concern should be its immediate neighborhood, including safeguarding U.S. borders, while remaining suspicious about security commitments such as NATO.[77]

- Accept that world order should be organized primarily through regional spheres of influence and that international agreements, organizations, and regimes have persistently undermined U.S. national interests.[78]

- Employ ultimatums in search of rapid diplomatic successes and threaten to walk away if demands are not met.[79]

- Consider the European Union a longtime adversary of the United States, while treating the leaders of China and Russia with personal warmth and professional respect.[80]

- Flatline or reduce defense spending and refuse to employ military force if it would produce substantial U.S. casualties.[81]

- Prevent the use or spread of nuclear weapons through verbal threats, diplomacy, and potentially force—if the conflict can be quickly resolved without American casualties or boots on the ground.[82]

- Reject U.S. government actions and international strategies regarding climate change and human rights.[83]

Defense of Trumpism

The heart of Trump's vision is that the liberal internationalist world order is irreparably broken because it is based on naïve assumptions—chief among them, the belief that international institutions, multilateral cooperation, and shared global norms can override raw power, national interests, and bilateral dealmaking.[84] Nations hustle, claw, and fight for power and influence, while ignoring international rules and norms that get in the way.[85] Therefore, there should be no long-term U.S. commitments and obligations, only a permanent quest for American advantage.[86] To the contrary, previous presidents have been hesitant to use the many instruments of U.S. power, especially economic threats to bludgeon acceptance of their preferred policies. Trumpism has ended that pusillanimous approach.

As Trump's allies see it, in the first year of his second term he has reestablished the United States as the globe's most powerful and influential nation.[87] He has strengthened the U.S. economy through high tariffs and a massive influx of foreign investment, stopped illegal immigration across the U.S. southern border, prevented or ended through his unique negotiating skill at least ten conflicts around the world, forced U.S. allies to finally pay their fair share of collective defense, and obliterated Iran's nuclear weapons programs.[88]

"Rather than pursuing a traditional establishment foreign policy, Trump is weighing all these international engagements through the lens of U.S. national security. In other words, he is guiding his policies on what will contribute to the security and prosperity of the American people rather than in pursuit of some abstract greater good," argued Victoria Coates of the Heritage Foundation, Trump's former deputy national security advisor.[89]

For Trumpism, trade is the cornerstone of U.S. national interests.[90] In Trump's view, global trade has gutted American manufacturing, and the imposition of tariffs and trade barriers is not just a tool of negotiation but a central requirement to redress the systemic inequities of previous trade policies.[91] He uses international crises as an opportunity for dealmaking and to elevate the U.S. global role under his singular leadership, but shrinks from employing military force that risks American casualties.[92]

The Trumpists conceive world order as largely composed of regional spheres of influence, in which great powers—the United States, China, and Russia—control their respective neighborhoods.[93] In the words of one commentator in October 2025, Trump portrays "the Western Hemisphere as America's natural sphere of destiny."[94] The leaders who deserve the most respect are not the heads of democracies in Europe and Asia but the two other sphere-of-influence principals, Chinese President Xi Jinping and Russian President Vladimir Putin.[95] NATO, the United Nations, and other international organizations inherently violate U.S. sovereignty and restrict American options and freedom of action in this belligerent world.[96]

Trump supporters assert that his grand strategy has chalked up notable successes. They argue that, as of December 2025, he has hammered out new trade arrangements with nine of the top fifteen U.S. trade partners, with more in the pipeline.[97] Trumpism proponents argue that after securing billion-dollar trade and investment agreements with Association of Southeast Asian Nations states, Japan, and South Korea during his October 2025 Asia tour, Trump also received concessions from China on soybeans, rare earths, and fentanyl restrictions.[98] In a major victory for Trump, the United States and EU agreed to a 15 percent tariff on EU goods imported to the United States but no tariffs on American exports to Europe.[99] The agreement also stipulates that the bloc will purchase $750 billion of American energy by 2028 and hundreds of billions of dollars of U.S. weapons.

His supporters contend that Trump's diplomatic and security policies have coerced NATO members to ramp up their defense spending (toward 5 percent of GDP), a long-held aim of successive U.S. administrations.[100] He has pledged $1 billion in vital weapons to Ukraine, paid for by European nations; pressured Russia to end the war; ended Iran's nuclear weapons program through his devastating attacks on the Fordow, Natanz, and Isfahan enrichment facilities; negotiated ceasefires between India and Pakistan, Israel and Iran, Cambodia and Thailand, and Rwanda and the Congo; and fostered an end of hostilities between Armenia and Azerbaijan.[101] And on November 19, 2025, he stated that he would make a new effort to end the war in Sudan.[102]

Trumpism proponents argue that one of Trump's most impressive feats was to broker a ceasefire between Israel and Hamas in October 2025—the best chance of peace in the Israel-Palestine conflict since the Oslo Accords.[103] After two years of fighting, the deal led to the release of all living Israeli hostages and a withdrawal of Israeli forces from nearly half the Gaza Strip.[104] Columnist Walter Russell Mead stressed the scale of that achievement: "Mr. Trump's genius was to find a framework within which these different powers with their different priorities could work together toward their common goal. It is a real accomplishment and deserves the world's gratitude and respect."[105] Indeed, that framework was then approved by the UN Security Council on November 17, 2025, another U.S. foreign policy victory.[106]

The strategist Hal Brands succinctly captures the Trump Doctrine, which "emphasizes using American power aggressively—more aggressively than Trump's immediate predecessors—to reshape key relationships and accrue U.S. advantage in a rivalrous world. In doing so, Trump has blown up any talk about a post-American era. . . . Several U.S. presidents pledged to use force to keep Tehran from crossing the nuclear threshold; Trump really did it."[107]

Critique of Trumpism

Critics argue that Trumpism constitutes a highly dangerous, personalized, and improvisational approach to U.S. foreign policy, molded by the impetuous temperament and autocratic political instincts of one individual.[108] Its essence is embedded in the personality of Trump and his thirst for renown, applause, and personal wealth.[109] Thus, he wades diplomatically into Ukraine, the Middle East, and South Asia (without experienced foreign policy experts) in a search for a Nobel Peace Prize and family commercial benefits.[110] Kissinger once warned, "any negotiator who seduces himself into believing that his personality leads to automatic breakthroughs will soon find himself in the special purgatory that history reserves for those who measure themselves by acclaim rather than achievement."[111] Trump appears not to have received the message.

According to the school's opponents, Trumpism asserts that one state's gain is necessarily at another's expense, that compromise is a fool's game, and that international rules and norms do not apply to him as the American president.[112] That attitude is bad for the United States, bad for the peace and prosperity of ordinary Americans, and bad for world order.[113]

The American-led international system created unprecedented mutual prosperity, which Trump would discard for a "might is right" world of dangerous uncertainty and conflict.[114] Critics opine that, with his theatrical bluster, empty threats, and erratic policies, Trump tarnishes Washington's image as a credible international actor, rattles allies, and heartens adversaries.[115] He purges experts on China and Russia from the intelligence community when the most serious threats come from those nations.[116] He decimates the leadership of the U.S. military.[117] He boasts that his negotiating skills have prevented or ended ten international crises, but can only name six, and many of those are suspect.[118] He orders attacks on ships in the Caribbean that purportedly carry drugs, actions which his critics contend are illegal or even war crimes, which former Secretary of Defense Leon Panetta charged on December 1, 2025.[119] He announces massive trade deals, most of which are only general frameworks with none of the details worked out—including those from his October 2025 Asia tour.[120] He asserts that in the context of those trade agreements, colossal private investment will flow to the United States even though most governments cannot force their firms to do so.[121] He claims that his foreign policy will put the United States first and not interfere in other countries' domestic affairs, even as he denounces the internal governance of nations ranging from Germany to South Africa, and in November 2025, he threatened to use force in Nigeria to protect Christians.[122]

Although there are those in the Trump administration who accurately view China as a security threat, such as Secretary of State Marco Rubio and Secretary of Defense Pete Hegseth, critics say Trump is blind to its growing economic, diplomatic, and military capabilities, its ratcheting pressure on Taiwan, its aggressive posture in the South China Sea, its influence operations abroad, and its ambition to revise global institutions at the expense of U.S. national interests.[123] For instance, by calling into question American treaty commitments, Trumpism fundamentally weakens extended deterrence and stirs debates in Japan and South Korea about acquiring nuclear weapons, or Trump's December 2025 decision to sell H200 advanced Nvidia chips to China, which his own Department of Justice called the "building blocks of AI superiority," and opponents say will undermine American leadership in the AI race.[124]

Critics argue that Trumpist economic nationalism is also fundamentally flawed. Trade deficits signal a strong service and tech sector, not weakness, and they result in part from the United States' highly beneficial privilege of issuing the world's reserve currency.[125] Meanwhile, as most economists argue, tariffs hurt U.S. consumers, manufacturers, farmers, American allies, and partners alike.[126] The United States thrives on the global ideas, people, and trade that Trump seeks to shut down.[127] Hoover Institution Senior Fellow Steven J. Davis described in October 2025 how the Trumpist approach to trade has created "a rupture in the international trading order that, despite its many flaws, fostered prosperity and security for more than eighty years."[128]

Opponents point out that, although Trump proclaims that the United States has the best military in the world, he has reduced the defense budget in real terms. Though headlines have widely reported that he has raised defense spending to $1 trillion, that figure reflects a one-time reconciliation bill and does not represent an increase to the baseline budget—which is a cut in real terms compared to Biden's term.[129] And for the first time in American history, under Trump, democratic values vanish from U.S. foreign policy. In his pathbreaking May 13, 2025, speech in Riyadh, Saudi Arabia, the president declared that "far too many American presidents have been afflicted with the notion that it's our job to look into the souls of foreign leaders and use U.S. policy to dispense justice for their sins. . . . I believe it is God's job to sit in judgment—my job [is] to defend America and to promote the fundamental interests of stability, prosperity, and peace."[130]

Most important, critics contend that Trump embodies the most serious threat to American constitutional democracy since the Civil War and thus undermines the fundamental basis for U.S. power projection and influence in the world.

RESOLUTE GLOBAL LEADERSHIP

Given the limitations of each of the alternative schools of grand strategy, a U.S. grand strategy grounded in primacy and liberal internationalism is best recalibrated to reflect the particular challenges of the era. Primacy's emphasis on preserving U.S. military superiority and liberal internationalism's focus on global engagement and international cooperation are crucial going forward, but the United States now needs to reconcile itself to a world in which American dominance no longer goes unchallenged. In short, a grand strategy of resolute global leadership enshrines Reagan's dictum "peace through strength" rather than attempting to attain peace through unipolar dominance, withdrawal, or bluster.

Enduring American Advantages

Although China has substantially reduced its strategic and tactical disadvantages vis-à-vis the United States in the past decade and a half, the U.S. grand strategy of resolute global leadership is moored to the United States' immense economic, military, and diplomatic power, both real and potential.

With a GDP of over $30 trillion, the United States has the largest economy in the world.[131] It not only has the globe's greatest concentration of material wealth but also enjoys extraordinary levels of distributed prosperity. With a per capita income of over $85,000 in 2024, Americans are far richer than the Chinese, whose per capita income is slightly more than $13,300.[132] The United States commands just over 26 percent of global GDP, the same share it did in the early 1990s; China's share peaked at 18.5 percent in 2021.[133] Since 2020, U.S. real GDP has grown by 10 percent, or triple the Group of Seven (G7) average.[134] Just under 58 percent of all foreign exchange reserves are held in U.S. dollars, which remains the world's primary reserve currency.[135] American labor productivity has soared by 70 percent since 1990, compared with 29 percent in Europe, 46 percent in Britain, and 25 percent in Japan.[136]

Despite concerns about the American industrial base, manufacturing contributed $2.3 trillion to U.S. GDP in 2023, and the United States has the second-largest manufacturing sector in the world (behind China), surpassing those of Germany, Japan, and South Korea combined.[137] In 2023, it channeled roughly $940 billion into research and development, the most of any nation.[138]

Although it is far too early to conclusively judge how the AI race between the United States and China will evolve, U.S. AI start-ups have amassed over $100 billion in 2025 through August alone, while Bank of America estimates that in 2025, Chinese public-private AI investment could crest at $98 billion.[139] The American AI titans secure more funding than those in China: for instance, OpenAI's Stargate Project has already acquired at least $100 billion and aims to raise $500 billion in private backing.[140] The four most accurate large language models, according to the most difficult standard of AI benchmarking analysts, are American-made.[141] The United States also commands 75 percent of global supercomputer capacity, stacked against China's 15 percent—a critical advantage in American AI infrastructure.[142] The United States produced forty notable AI models in 2024 according to Stanford University's AI Index Report, compared with China's fifteen.[143] And despite China's efforts to transition its companies to domestic semiconductor providers, the country's most successful AI model (DeepSeek) still relies on American Nvidia chips for training.[144]

Since 2019, the United States has been a net energy exporter, and in 2024, it exported roughly 30 percent of the energy it produced—about $332 billion in revenue.[145] That provides Washington with critical leverage. It allows the United States to reduce its energy dependence, as well as the dependence of allies, on an unstable Middle East, and since 2022, Europe has accounted for over half of all American liquid natural gas exports as European states lessen their reliance on Russian energy.[146]

Moreover, according to the 2025 Times World University Rankings, seven of the top ten universities are American.[147] The United States attracts far more foreign researchers than any other country, delivering major innovation benefits: since 2000, immigrants to the United States have won 40 percent of the Nobel Prizes awarded to Americans in chemistry, physics, and medicine.[148] The United States also tops the list of countries with the highest number of highly cited researchers, with 36.4 percent of the global total against China's 22.3 percent in 2024.[149]

Thanks to its powerful economy, the United States deploys the most formidable military in the world, with a $849 billion defense budget for fiscal year (FY) 2025.[150] U.S. defense spending constitutes 37 percent of global military expenditures and exceeds the next nine countries combined (see figure 1).[151] In FY 2025, the Pentagon will allocate $141 billion on research—roughly

FIGURE 1

U.S. Military Spending Exceeds That of China and Russia Combined

Military spending by country, constant 2023 dollars

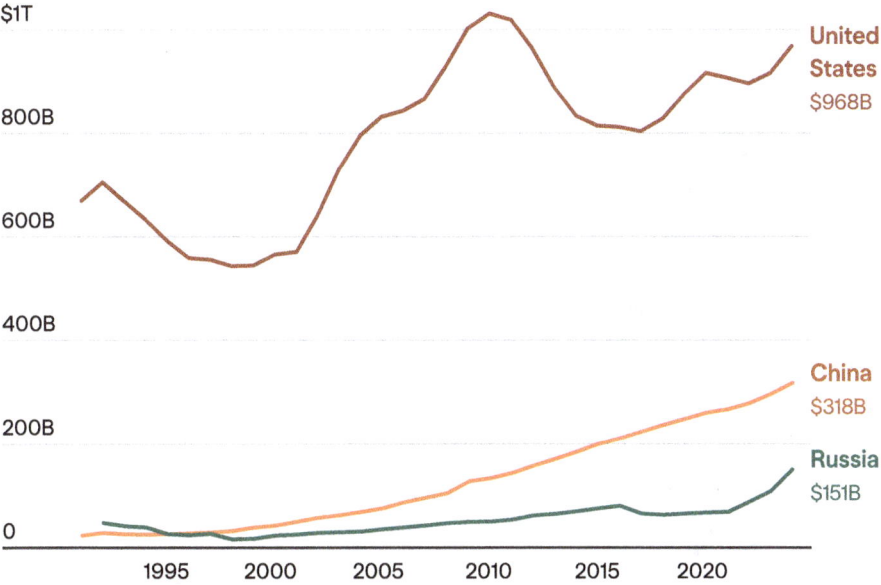

Source: Stockholm International Peace Research Institute

equivalent to Russia's entire defense budget.[152] It remains the world's leading military equipment manufacturer, accounting for about 43 percent of arms exports in 2024, with five of the ten largest arms producers.[153]

The United States wields a nuclear triad—land-based intercontinental ballistic missiles, submarine-launched ballistic missiles, and nuclear-capable strategic bombers—of around 1,700 deployed strategic nuclear weapons, with a secure second-strike capability.[154] It marshals 2.1 million military personnel—including over 1.4 million in the army—with almost 400,000 armored vehicles, over 100,000 more than China and Russia combined.[155] It fields the world's largest and most advanced air force with over 13,000 aircraft, more than the next 4 largest air forces (China, Russia, India, and

South Korea) combined.[156] It deploys the most state-of-the-art navy, the largest in tonnage and second largest (after China) in number of vessels, including 11 aircraft carriers and 71 nuclear-powered submarines.[157] It operates 750 military bases in at least 80 countries, approximately 247 military satellites, and a sophisticated Cyber Command.[158] Its intelligence agencies influence and penetrate governments around the globe.[159]

The United States has also harnessed lethal AI systems more effectively than China. As American defense contractors such as RTX, Anduril, and Palantir design and produce next-generation drones and AI for warfare, the Pentagon's Replicator Initiative aims to provide thousands of autonomous drones and robotic systems across air, land, and sea domains within an eighteen-to-twenty-four-month timeline.[160] Chinese academics frequently bemoan how they trail the United States in military uses of AI.[161]

Based on that enormous economic and military power, American diplomatic reach, in principle and if skillfully applied, outstrips that of any other country. The United States is virtually always the prime negotiating intermediary around the world to try to prevent, end, or suspend conflict—in recent times, between Russia and Ukraine, Israel and Hamas, India and Pakistan, Rwanda and Democratic Republic of Congo, Cambodia and Thailand, and Armenia and Azerbaijan.[162] (Beijing has had a fraction of Washington's diplomatic sway over the actors in any of those confrontations.)

With major influence over most of the region's actors, the United States holds the dominant diplomatic position in the Middle East—as seen in the 2020 Abraham Accords, its attempts to broker rapprochement between Israel and Saudi Arabia, its close ties to the United Arab Emirates and Qatar, its efforts to coax the new Syrian government toward responsible international behavior, its diplomacy to reestablish productive ties with Turkey, and its intense work to ostracize Iran.[163]

In Europe, the United States has singular influence over NATO and the European Union, as they often follow its lead, most recently in response to the 2022 Russian full-scale invasion of Ukraine and to transatlantic alignment on China policy.[164] Similarly, the United States has the preeminent position in the Indo-Pacific, buttressed by allies Australia, Japan, the Philippines, and South Korea, as well as the Quad coalition of the United States, Australia, India, and Japan.[165] The United States is also an institutional leader, occupying the central position of influence at the World Bank, G7, and the Group of Twenty, as well as veto power in the UN Security Council. And the United States has traditionally possessed not merely its raw strength but rather the acquiescence, if not consent, of large portions of the world to its policy preferences.[166]

Meanwhile, Beijing's ambitions are undercut by problems at home. The National Bureau of Statistics reported that China's economy expanded by the suspiciously exact official target of 5 percent in 2024, but the independent Rhodium Group estimates growth was between 2.4 and 2.8 percent, which would mark one of the worst years for GDP growth since the death of People's Republic of China founder and leader Mao Zedong in 1976.[167] China's debt ratio surged from 150 percent of GDP in the late 2000s to over 300 percent of its GDP in 2024, as many Chinese real estate developers struggled to stay afloat.[168] Its youth unemployment rate remains stubbornly high at nearly 18 percent as of September 2025, even after Beijing altered its methodology in an attempt to lower the number.[169] China's demographic profile deteriorated in the aftermath of its one-child policy, with its population growth declining 94 percent between 2011 and 2021, the working-age population rapidly dwindling, and the median age of its citizens climbing.[170] Even after China announced a three-child policy in 2021, its fertility rate has remained alarmingly low—at 1.0 as of 2024 (far below the 2.1 replacement rate).[171] In 2024, the United Nations predicted that the Chinese population will decline by 43 percent from 1.4 billion today to 633 million in 2100.[172] As CFR Senior Fellow Sebastian Mallaby has observed, "You have to go back to the plagues and famines of the late medieval period to find a loss of population so severe."[173] That plummeting Chinese population, coupled with an increasing old-age dependency ratio, will further weaken China's economy over the long term and thus the foundation of its power projection.[174]

China has suffered military problems as well.[175] The People's Liberation Army (PLA) struggles with an untested command structure and insufficient joint operations capabilities, while its defense industry remains dependent on the United States and its partners for critical high-tech imports.[176] China's armed forces also face issues of corruption among the top brass and lower-level officials as Xi has called for an "early warning mechanism for integrity risks in the military."[177] Nine senior generals were expelled on October 17, 2025, on charges of corruption and abuses of power, the largest public military crackdown in decades.[178] The purge removed the powerful vice chairman of the Central Military Commission and the commander of the Eastern Theater—the regional command most important to any war over Taiwan.[179]

Such purges have harmed the PLA's readiness for combat.[180] According to Bloomberg, sources in the U.S. intelligence community report that "corruption inside China's Rocket Force and throughout the nation's defense industrial base is so extensive that U.S. officials now believe Xi is less likely to contemplate major military action in the coming years than would otherwise have been the case."[181] Other defense deficiencies affect China's goal of integrating Taiwan, including insufficient numbers of large amphibious ships, a lack of combat experience for a military that has not seen conflict since the 1979 land war with Vietnam, mediocre capabilities in carrier operations and submarine stealth, and an inadequate supply of skilled recruits for its booming fleet.[182]

Given the reality of the United States' unique international strengths and China's profound weaknesses, U.S. grand strategy can chart only one of two directions. Washington could enact destructive policies that diminish its power and influence. In a world of highly competitive international politics and a hostile peer rival, such a choice would be bizarre, but the policy prescriptions of the restraint, American nationalism, and Trumpism schools have precisely that effect.

Which leaves only the second alternative: to restore and apply American power. That approach is best exemplified by the grand strategy of resolute global leadership, rather than primacy, which fails to recognize China as a peer competitor, or liberal internationalism, which is overly reliant on international institutions to advance American vital national interests and underestimates the importance of military power in a competitive world order. If that is the sole surviving responsible option, the principal aim of U.S. grand strategy should be to consciously consolidate and skillfully apply the extraordinary power and influence of its structural strengths, and especially to reverse its dangerously inadequate response to the rise of Chinese power. The superiority of resolute global leadership as a grand strategy is evident in how effectively it fulfills the three criteria by which strategies should be judged: greater prosperity, improved security, and stronger legitimacy.

Sustaining Prosperity

The United States' ability to reestablish a sturdy international system hinges on its capacity to sustain a flourishing economy. Maintaining the potency of the U.S. economy depends on preserving its efficiency in allocating the factors of production, and there is no better instrument for that purpose than free markets at home supervised by an effective state able to correct market failures and advance the common good. With a highly efficient economic system, U.S. companies are almost always first or early movers in disruptive technologies, including AI and quantum computers.[183] That dominance produces supernormal returns that both increase the country's standard of living and facilitate its superior military.

The U.S. economic system outclasses other nations, but its domestic market is not large enough to adequately consume all the goods it produces. Therefore, U.S. policymakers after the Second World War forged a relatively open global trading system so that the American economy could benefit from enlarged markets beyond its national frontiers.[184] (Geopolitical considerations obviously played an important role too, as trade helped the war-torn economies of Asia and Europe speedily recover and thus better resist communism.[185]) Those markets expanded the efficiencies of a division of labor that previously occurred primarily only within the United States to new territories abroad.[186]

As a result, manufacturing, which was once an American specialty, steadily migrated to other locales such as China and the other East Asian Tigers. The United States remained a net beneficiary, however, as the returns from expanded foreign trade raised the purchasing power of American consumers across the board.[187] The shift in manufacturing abroad provided lower-cost goods for the U.S. public at home, who, as a result, have morphed into the world's largest consumer market and an important driver of global demand.[188]

It is now well established that countries that dominate the leading technological sectors of an age either become its major powers or preserve their position at the top.[189] Because the United States possesses a prodigious "national innovation system," it is well positioned to lead the emerging high-tech industries.[190] The factors that underwrite that leverage are in many ways unique to the United States, and traditionally include a deeply competitive and highly flexible market system; an entrepreneurial culture resilient in the face of failure; a large venture capital pool; a vibrant research-and-development ecosystem that encompasses world-class universities; a vast private sector; significant governmental support for innovation; a robust regulatory framework that enshrines the rule of law, sanctity of contracts, and the protection of intellectual property; and highly skilled and talented labor at all levels of the productive enterprise.[191] The global power, influence, and values of the United States in the postwar period have been its best calling card, serving to attract foreign capital, skills, and collaboration in ways that have crucially enhanced U.S. national interests.

Although that remarkable regime has enriched the country in the aggregate, it has imposed transitional costs on different slices of the population, as when the "China shock" of the 2000s dislodged sections of the laboring class involved in mass manufacturing.[192] The gradual transformation of the United States into a knowledge economy also heaped burdens on those Americans who are not well educated and were less able to take advantage of, as sociologist Daniel Bell put it, "knowledge, for the purpose of social control and the directing of innovation and change."[193]

The current turmoil in American politics represented by the rise of Donald Trump is driven in part (if the cultural roots of contemporary resentment are excluded) by a desire to rectify the failings of the U.S. political system to support those buffeted by the transformations wrought by trade, automation, and the growing knowledge centricity of the American economy.[194] Confronting those problems, which the United States needs to address to protect the material foundations of its international influence, requires considered policies. Those cannot consist, however, of broadsides against the international trading system, assaults on immigration, challenges to the rule of law, slashes in federal funding for basic and advanced research, and attacks on universities and other national incubators of groundbreaking scientific and technological discoveries, which all weaken the building blocks of innovation and, by extension, prosperity.[195]

Those counterproductive responses have erupted at a moment when China has emerged as a powerful and sophisticated peer rival with an alternative model of technological progress, one that, according to Chinese-auto-industry expert Michael Dunne, "combines government financial support, methodical long-term planning and aggressive innovation" to produce world-class industries that could eclipse their American counterparts as the fountainhead of knowledge production.[196] Unlike the Soviet Union—which possessed insignificant technological prowess outside the military sector—China is a formidable economic competitor.[197]

Although some seek to ape China when they institute industrial policy at home and wreck the international trading system abroad, such efforts will not help Washington compete with Beijing.[198] There are compelling reasons, however, to reconfigure the current pattern of globalization to protect the critical supply chains of national defense, specialized raw materials, and public health, complemented by more stringent export controls on critical technologies flowing to China, Iran, North Korea, Russia, and other foes.[199]

By sustaining an open society and an open economy that engages in international commerce with the widest set of trading partners, Washington will possess inherent systemic advantages in its contest with Beijing: openness secures access to critical assets, multiplies the sources of innovation, and means that while Beijing can mobilize state power, Washington can take advantage of the dynamism of a far wider global network.[200] The alternatives of statism, autarky, and mercantilism, which the Trump administration lionizes in its pursuit of bilateral trade deals, fall woefully short in terms of growing the global economy, boosting the U.S. share of it, and maximizing American material and thus strategic power.[201]

Economic prosperity requires global trade integration, efficient markets, and well-designed domestic policies that support innovation and protect those affected by economic change. The United States can also increase American prosperity through deeper trade ties with emerging economies in which foreign middle classes desire American goods and services. At home, the best course for the United States is to safeguard the rule of law, fortify its institutional structures, retool its regulatory systems, and sustain its open society to make markets as efficient as possible, while strengthening the safety nets that help those jostled by the markets' continual adjustments.[202] Moreover, the United States should focus on research and development. That type of spending delivers the largest long-run returns because new knowledge spills across firms, compounds over time, and seeds entire industries. There is a role for limited state activism—which could include, as a report by the Information Technology and Innovation Foundation recommended, initiatives such as increasing research-and-development tax credits or establishing a new advanced research projects agency, which translates into prosperity through lower after-tax costs and decreased risk from innovation.[203]

Enhancing Security

The stability of world order and the success of Washington require the United States to increase its extraordinary power projection abroad. After all, the nation cannot pursue its multifarious interests at home or abroad if its territory and its people are threatened by attack. Ringed by friendly (and weaker) neighbors to its north and south and by vast oceans to its east and west, the continental United States already enjoys enviable protection.[204]

If any other country had chanced into such secure geography, it would have considered itself remarkably lucky. Not surprisingly, many strands of

American nationalist and Trumpist schools brand international engagement as largely dispensable because the nation is safe within its borders and can afford to be indifferent to distant developments.

Unfortunately, the geography of the United States (even if considered only in its continental dimension) is insufficient to preserve its physical security. When American national interests are superimposed upon its geography, the country is not as invulnerable as it first appears. In an age when weapons have intercontinental reach and when U.S. rivals possess such catastrophic instruments, the well-being bestowed by geography is highly porous. Cyber capabilities make that fact even clearer: attacks launched from anywhere on the globe can potentially penetrate U.S. financial networks, critical infrastructure, and military command systems in seconds. Those realities undercut the argument of restraint advocates who claim that oceans shield the United States from danger.

Moreover, U.S. strategic responsibilities today extend vitally to the defense of its far-flung allies and are no longer limited to its home and outlying territories alone. To shield those allies is not to give American alms to foreign beggars. Rather, it allows the United States to mobilize coalitions to confront acute and chronic dangers.[205] Over time, the United States has harnessed confederations of like-minded states to serve multiple aims: to exploit their requisite geographic advantages, to magnify U.S. military strength against common adversaries, to reap the benefits of legitimacy deriving from multiple partners wedded to common causes, and to blunt the challenges that could be posed by members of its own syndicates were they to stand independent of the United States.[206]

Those diverse advantages of U.S. alliances and strong partnerships are often missed when they are viewed exclusively through the lens of burden sharing. Driven by that narrow view, the claim that U.S. allies need to match the United States' military contributions to ensure an effective common defense has surged in popularity. If allies were independent militarily, however, that would likely undermine American influence over those partners. Far from remaining beneficiaries of American protection, they could decouple in ways that would potentially not serve long-term U.S. interests.[207]

Thus, the United States should cajole allies to increase defense spending, but not to the extent that would permit them to shed their reliance on the country nor confidently oppose U.S. national interests. The U.S. alliance system aims to accumulate the capabilities necessary to defend and promote U.S. national interests, defeat common threats, and secure

American leadership. For instance, were Europe freed from dependence on Washington's NATO Article 5 security guarantee, it would be more likely to adopt policies at odds with U.S. preferences and more acutely feel China's already-strong gravitational pull on trade, climate, global health, and even Taiwan.

The U.S. economy is still bigger than the economies of the thirty European members of NATO combined.[208] In the Indo-Pacific region, the comparison is even more lopsided: the U.S. economy is over three times larger than the Australian, Japanese, Philippine, and South Korean economies combined.[209]

The bottom line is clear: while there are trade-offs, the United States can afford to increase its larger contributions to collective defense to preserve its extraordinary influence, and it can do so without impoverishing its population. Seeking greater allied contributions makes sense: it increases combined military capabilities, it promotes greater allied responsibilities, it broadcasts to adversaries that the allies are willing to bear burdens to protect their security, and it soothes the complaints of U.S. domestic constituencies who accuse the allies of free riding.[210] But as the data already indicates, the frequent accusations that American treaty allies are free riders in collective defense are consistently exaggerated.[211] Thus, aiming for equal contributions is both quixotic (given the disparity in U.S. and allied economic strength) and perilous to the defense of American global leadership and influence.

Once one accepts that allies lie at the core of U.S. grand strategy, two other goals emerge as essential to American security: to preserve favorable balances of power in critical regions of the world and to defuse threats far from the American homeland.[212]

There are four centers of gravity in the international system where the United States has vital national interests. Each is marked by large concentrations of economic, technological, and military power. The most important area is obviously the United States' own hemisphere, which the nation has historically shielded from great-power contests and external security threats.[213] Beyond the Americas, however, the United States has sought to ensure that the vast Eurasian landmass is never subdued by any hostile power that could mobilize its resources against the New World.[214] That has translated into commitments throughout Europe, the Indo-Pacific rimland, and the greater Middle East, trip wires that trigger American intervention whenever a single state threatens to dominate an entire region.

The formal alliances that the United States maintains in Europe and in East Asia and the de facto alliances in the Middle East ensure those regions remain zones of American power and influence and not territories subjugated to China, Iran, North Korea, or Russia. Since the end of the Second World War, those security arrangements have rightly counted as the foundation blocks of the U.S.-led world order. They enable the United States to resist its adversaries closer to their homelands rather than within the American hemisphere, while mobilizing the resources of its allies to collectively forestall the ambitions of various adversaries. Absent those arrangements, the United States would have to oppose such threats independently or rely at best on transient coalitions, which do not guarantee durable security.[215]

The preservation of permanent confederacies requires allies and partners that remain aligned with the United States and an American readiness to compromise. Neither arises by nature. While allies responsibly contribute toward collective defense, Washington should seriously consider their policy preferences, which have been too often ignored.[216] But it is even more important that the United States sustain a comprehensive military superiority over its adversaries to checkmate its rivals in their own backyards and defend its allies in situ, thereby protecting the United States without depending entirely on homeland defense.

Military superiority should be coupled with sound technology controls. Because both economic and geopolitical success depend on choking off opponents' easy access to critical technologies, even within an otherwise open trading system, the United States cannot afford to assault its allies and partners more than it confronts its adversaries.[217] Failing to grasp the fundamental difference between friends and foes sets the United States on a path where it could shed the former without defeating the latter, in both the arena of trade and the profound realm of geopolitics.

The greatest long-term threat to the security of the United States and its partners is, of course, China. As a result, the United States should redeploy military forces to Asia from Europe and the Middle East—without vacating either—to stifle China's hegemonic ambitions in the Indo-Pacific and beyond. That approach would entail a reengineered division of labor: European and Middle Eastern allies take point in regional defense with the United States offering robust backup, while in Asia, the United States and its allies there, bolstered by new and expanded capabilities, would concentrate on that region.[218] Along with those modifications, Washington should intensify U.S. diplomacy with Beijing to avoid war, which will require compromise on both sides, and collaborate with China to address global problems such as climate change, terrorism, illegal drugs, and pandemics.[219]

Cementing Legitimacy

The United States possesses a unique global reach and capabilities thanks to its large, vibrant, and innovative economy. Successful U.S. policies over time also need sufficient international legitimacy, however—a general acceptance by its allies and partners of the validity of Washington's international objectives and the strategies to achieve them. Those collaborators support and thus legitimize American policy based not only on its merits but also on the exceptional American power and influence in the world that underpin them.[220]

The importance of securing legitimacy derives from inequality in the global system. Since international politics is a competitive realm, the immensity of American power can menace the interests of states that, depending on their own national capabilities, would perhaps rally against the United States on their own or with others.[221] That process of balancing is neither automatic nor instantaneous, and it can be arrested by the behavior of the larger power. A stronger state employing blatant and persistent force against weaker ones can accelerate the balancing behavior of smaller countries. But artful international conduct—one that provides benefits systemwide, espouses an attractive ideology, and restricts force—can elicit acquiescence and even consent.[222]

Given the significant power asymmetries in favor of the United States, a grand strategy of resolute global leadership prioritizes making American advantages palatable to the largest number of countries. That covers, at minimum, Washington's myriad allies, but should also encompass as many of the "nonaligned" nations as possible. If Washington succeeds on that count, this grand strategy will magnetize the support of most states, except for a small number of inveterate foes.

U.S. policymakers intuitively valued international legitimacy during the Cold War because they understood that the contest was not simply a military, technological, and economic competition but an ideological one as well.[223] That was welcome news for the United States, as it was advancing an attractive vision of world order. It respected sovereign states; set out to raise prosperity through the expansion of foreign assistance programs, free markets at home, and open trade abroad; and created and cultivated a diverse set of international institutions that collectively sought the peaceful resolution of disputes in a well-ordered global system.[224]

Although U.S. practices often departed from those ideals, their stark contrast to the worldview espoused by Soviet communism ensured American normative dominance for more than four decades. Both Soviet communism and liberal internationalism envisioned a hopeful future, but Soviet communism imploded because its intellectual foundations proved unable to sustain the necessary productive economic base. In parallel, Moscow's naked imperialism could not contain both the realities of nationalism in the Soviet republics and the desire for freedom on the part of its east European client states.[225]

Despite periodic blemishes, liberal internationalism thrived because of superior and diverse American power, and because the United States championed an open international system. Emphasizing the sanctity of inalienable individual rights that flourish in elected governments with limited power, the global security order upheld the stability of state boundaries, untangled interstate disagreements through negotiation rather than war, and sponsored varied organizations to help manage international interactions in both high and low politics. The trading system steadily expanded international commerce and erected a nondiscriminatory system of tariff reductions and structured dispute resolution. The financial order focused on sustaining the stability of the international monetary system and poverty reduction through loans and technical assistance. And the nonproliferation regime successfully prevented the use of nuclear weapons and markedly slowed their spread.

The collective success of this liberal international order opened its doors to all states, irrespective of their capabilities, and offered the possibility of peaceful change despite ever-present rivalries.[226] As fresh challenges surfaced, such as public health and climate change, the international regimes created since the Second World War multiplied to address them.

But it bears repeating that, although the liberal international order relied on the mutual interest of states for its long-term success, it could not have been brought into existence, or endured over its many decades, without the overwhelming power of the United States. Only the United States could bear the exceptional costs required to keep such a system aloft.[227]

In contemporary U.S. domestic politics, the price of upholding the liberal international order is often cast as a waste of national resources or as an unrequited favor bestowed upon undeserving states.[228] Those sentiments are understandable given that many nations that benefit from U.S. power sometimes pursue policies that undermine American aims—Saudi Arabia took the lead in imposing an oil embargo on the United States during the Yom Kippur War, while protected by U.S. force of arms; for decades, Europe sheltered behind American military strength while pursuing trade policies at U.S. expense; and India has purchased discounted Russian oil, which strengthens Russia's combative objectives in Ukraine, while depending on the United States to balance the rise of Chinese power. But defending the liberal international order is fundamentally in U.S. national interests because it cements the legitimacy of U.S. power. The United States' singular ability to provide collective goods that benefit all, as well as those additional goods it extends to its friends and allies, induced much of the world for more than half a century to make peace with American strength.[229]

The creation of those public goods carries advantages beyond legitimacy; they flow back into U.S. coffers as material gains.[230] Their absence would accelerate the proliferation of nuclear weapons, ignite wars for territorial aggrandizement, and intensify the chaos and consequences of financial crises—all threats that would imperil the United States directly. The United States undoubtedly pays more and risks more than others to maintain the various regimes that help prevent such outcomes, but it does so because, as the most powerful state, it has the most to lose if the larger system were to crumble around it. Consequently, bearing the costs to buttress the world order, especially when Washington can afford it better than others, is essential.

To fully reap the benefits of legitimacy, the United States has three obligations. First, it should furnish public goods that help the world at large. The absence of those goods, with consequences such as increased threats to freedom of navigation or the proliferation of nuclear weapons, will create greater incentives for other states to ignore American interests, thus raising the costs of exercising U.S. influence globally.[231]

Second, the United States should treat its allies and partners respectfully and factor their national interests into its policies. For the most part, Washington is graced with close associates who are relatively wealthy and who, being part of the political and strategic West, converge on a common vision of world order. Consequently, those states are willing to contribute to the upkeep of various global regimes that benefit themselves and the United States.

Third, the United States should fund and uphold liberal norms at home and abroad to bolster world order. The uniqueness of the American-led liberal international order consists of the United States' willingness to bind itself to certain universal rules in exchange for international acceptance of its centrality and privileges.[232] That does not imply that the United States is always condemned to accept international preferences if they harm its vital national interests. But it does require Washington to be much more sensitive to how it exercises power, especially military force. Force is only acceptable if it represents an inescapable choice to protect vital national interests. Promoting democracy is never such an inescapable American choice.

Pillars of Resolute Global Leadership

The eleven pillars of resolute global leadership are as follows:

- Preserve and protect the American constitutional order.

- Maintain American military superiority and the willingness to use force on behalf of vital U.S. national interests by substantially increasing the defense budget over the next decade and winning the high-technology race with China, especially in artificial intelligence.

- Revitalize and reform a rules-based world order through sustained American leadership and intense diplomacy to advance the viability and stability of major global systems and institutions for trade, financial markets, freedom of the seas, energy, space, and health.

- Prevent the use and spread of nuclear weapons, including through force.

- Stave off China's hegemonic objectives by pivoting U.S. military forces to Asia from Europe and the Middle East, strengthening American alliances, leading the collaborative reform of the international trading system, and taking seriously the views and needs of the developing world.

- Demand that U.S. allies and partners in Europe and the Middle East play a prominent role in their regional security and deterrence with substantially increased defense spending, supported by continual and comprehensive American military and diplomatic backup.

- Intensify U.S. diplomacy with China to avoid war over Taiwan, while collaborating with China to address global problems such as the climate, international terrorism, illegal drugs, and pandemics.

- Increase diplomatic and economic engagement with the Western Hemisphere, especially the Arctic passage, the Caribbean, and North America, through additional trade agreements with an emphasis on supply chains for critical minerals, semiconductors, and energy.

- Defend vigorously democracy and human rights around the world, without the use of military force except to avert genocide.

- Treat climate change as a profound global threat requiring multilateral cooperation, binding international agreements, and U.S. leadership in environmental standards.

- Encourage governmental frameworks and incentives that stimulate healthy, transnational private actors on behalf of U.S. national interests.

ASSESSING RESOLUTE GLOBAL LEADERSHIP AGAINST ITS ALTERNATIVES

The notion of resolute global leadership is rooted in the tradition of pragmatic realism that marked postwar U.S. policy. Because it assumes a conflictual global system, the approach holds that preponderant U.S. power, including military power, is indispensable for protecting the United States and its allies.[233] It recognizes the limitations of international institutions and the necessity of military tools—although force should always be used wisely, sparingly, and overwhelmingly when necessary.

Resolute global leadership has much in common with primacy. Both hammer home that U.S. influence in the world rests on the global projection of military power, which is the foundation for American economic and diplomatic fortunes. Both schools emphasize the need to shore up major global systems, such as alliances and global trading institutions. Both oppose the use and spread of weapons of mass destruction, especially nuclear weapons, including by force. Both back pivoting U.S. military forces to Asia while retaining substantial capabilities in Europe and the Middle East. Both support a rigorous technology control regime to cease the outward flow of advanced technologies to U.S. adversaries and reduce supply chain vulnerabilities in defense, critical minerals, and public health. Both emphasize that the United States should strengthen alliances and bilateral partnerships to deal with global problems. And both urge the United States to mind its neighborhood and collaborate more with partners in the Western Hemisphere.

The main difference between the two schools is that resolute global leadership accepts that the United States now has China as a peer competitor, whereas primacists believe the United States should be unrivaled in every region. Though primacists would employ American power regardless of whether they enlisted the support of partners, the United States must now draw on the strength of allies and partners to compete with China. America alone is likely America defeated.[234] In addition, the two grand strategies diverge on whether to deploy military force for ideological goals such as promoting human rights and democracy. Unlike primacy, the grand strategy of resolute global leadership rejects military force to obtain those objectives, except to prevent genocide.

Of course, if preventing a peer competitor from emerging had been possible, both schools would have rejoiced. But given that the rise of China is now an indisputable fact, resolute global leadership emphasizes the need to balance China's power rather than seek to overthrow its regime.[235] Military, diplomatic, economic, and technological balancing in response to China's substantial gains over the last fifteen years requires resolute allies and partners, and as much support as possible from developing nations across the globe.

Although it shares some perspectives with liberal internationalism—support for international institutions, the multilateral trading system, climate action, deeper engagement with the developing world, backing for NATO and Ukraine, and a place for American values in foreign policy—the grand strategy of resolute global leadership also differs in important ways. It contends that military power is still central to competitive geopolitics and cannot be replaced by multilateral organizations, and thus calls for substantially increased U.S. defense spending. It foresees that the era ahead will be bipolar and not multipolar. It treats global institutions as important but instrumental: they count insofar as they advance U.S. national interests. It stresses that international bodies do not arise spontaneously but are forged and sustained by superior American power. It would defend Taiwan. It would employ military force to stop Iran from quickly acquiring a nuclear weapon through large stockpiles of highly enriched uranium.[236]

In the aftermath of the TPP fiasco, some liberal internationalists (like American nationalists and Trumpists) increasingly declare that the multilateral trade regime is dead.[237] That would surprise the nations that make up the Comprehensive and Progressive Agreement for Trans-Pacific Partnership (CPTPP)—Australia, Brunei, Canada, Chile, Japan, Malaysia, Mexico, New Zealand, Peru, Singapore, the United Kingdom, and Vietnam.[238] Signatories saw an increase in intra-CPTPP trade of 5.5 percent from 2018 to 2021.[239] China applied to join in September 2021, and experts estimate CPTPP membership will increase China's GDP by up to an additional 2.27 percent and its exports by up to 10.25 percent.[240] The irony is hard to overstate: the members of an agreement principally promoted by the United States to advance multilateral international trade now debate whether to permit entry to peer competitor and adversary China, while the United States stands aside.

Thus, as some pronounce the multilateral trade system purportedly buried, the rest of the world raises Lazarus. On top of the 2018 CPTPP, in 2019 the African Continental Free Trade Area was established as the largest free-trade area by number of member states after the World Trade Organization.[241] The Regional Comprehensive Economic Partnership entered into force in 2022 to aid trade between Indo-Pacific states that encompass 30 percent of global GDP and 28 percent of world trade.[242] Overall, 375 regional trade agreements are in force in 2025, compared to just 83 in 2000—a 352 percent increase.[243]

All that is occurring because the economic benefits of plurilateral agreements far exceed those of bilateral deals, since the former can accommodate the complex, multicountry production networks of modern manufacturing and services.[244] Global value chains (GVCs), which are especially suited to multilateral trade deals, account for roughly 70 percent of all international trade, and economists estimate that a 1 percent increase in GVC participation boosts per capita income levels by more than 1 percent.[245] In addition, so-called plurilateral deals—adding signatories to existing bilateral agreements—which the naysayers prescribe as an alternative to multilateral agreements, are nothing new.[246] The United States has combined bilateral with regional and multilateral accords for at least fifty years, including the original Trans-Pacific Partnership, which was built on earlier bilateral free-trade agreements.[247]

In short, the old system is not dead. It continues in arrangements, rules, standards, and norms that have facilitated international commerce for decades and produced a 4,500 percent growth in trade volume since 1950.[248] High-quality bilateral, plurilateral, and regional accords—anchored in an international trading system with the United States at its nucleus to guide, expand, and integrate agreements—will best advance American interests under a reformed and revitalized World Trade Organization.[249] A liberal internationalist president should articulate a convincing defense of a reformed trading system to the American people.

Alongside its inability to uphold the international trading system, contemporary liberal internationalism failed to adequately respond to the rise of China. For fifteen years, as China ratcheted up its power and influence in Asia, the United States combined increasingly hostile rhetoric with limp policies. American defense spending as a share of GDP trended down from 2010, with far too little enhanced power projection.[250] The U.S. pivot from other regions to Asia was a figment of the White House's imagination.[251] American economic leadership in the Indo-Pacific disappeared.[252] Paltry reactions from U.S. leaders encouraged a dangerous Chinese conviction that the United States was in long-term decline, distracted and divided, systemically unable to guard its vital national interests. Across the Indo-Pacific, friendly nations reluctantly began to draw similarly bleak conclusions and worried about U.S. commitments, reliability, and staying power.[253] And all that occurred before Trump's second term.

The other three alternative grand strategies fail even more consequentially than contemporary liberal internationalism. Restraint advances two contestable assumptions. First, it wagers that the United States is sufficiently secure within its own geography and does not need international entanglements to protect its national interests. Second, it asserts that even if the rise of a peer challenger poses a threat to the United States, the nation should simply rely on the balancing by regional powers that will supposedly convene to block those dangers. If an aggressor threatened to overrun regional players, some versions of the restraint doctrine would have the United States station offshore forces that would thunder down like the U.S. cavalry to rescue partners at the last moment.[254]

Resolute global leadership rejects those assumptions. Although the United States is geographically advantaged relative to others, it is vulnerable to over-the-horizon attacks. While American military strength can deter and mitigate such dangers, it is not foolproof and needs to be supplemented by resilient forward forces. Alliances and foreign deployments reflect the reality that geopolitical balancing often fails—a phenomenon that creates great empires. Should that occur, the security challenges facing the United States would arise closer to home and grow tougher to combat.[255]

Hence, an American forward military presence is crucial in East Asia, Europe, and the Middle East. The restraint school sometimes endorses a suitably minimized defense of Asia and Europe but scoffs at the need for American defense in the Middle East given that the United States is no longer dependent on energy imports from that region. Even if the considerations of defending Israel and the moderate Gulf monarchies are discounted, the Middle East still contains vast energy resources that U.S. competitors could dominate, a reality that justifies U.S. military protection and diplomatic attention. It would be reckless to completely divest American power and influence in the region.

Restraint provides a sensible reminder that the United States should apportion resources wisely and avoid futile military adventures, but it ignores the linkages between the United States' global military presence, its guardianship of world order, and the viability of the international trading system. All of those elements promote peace and stability by attenuating regional security dilemmas and knitting together the productive economic ties that enrich Americans and others.[256] Although the costs of those obligations fall largely to the United States, it remains well within the country's ability to purchase the public goods that enhance its influence.

American nationalism suffers from similar weaknesses. Taken to its logical conclusion, that approach would be satisfied so long as the United States is safe and prosperous in its own local environs, with its legitimacy being largely irrelevant to those limited national interests.[257] As long as other great powers do not contest the country's hemispheric dominance, American nationalism is comfortable with other major powers establishing their own spheres of influence elsewhere.[258] U.S. prosperity in that conception is protected through the country's own economic engines and bilateral trade agreements with other states.

Resolute global leadership rejects American nationalism on the grounds that it posits a highly truncated conception of the U.S. role in the world, one that takes little advantage of its standing as the most powerful nation. The United States acquired that status after painful experiences of defeating other great powers that imperiled U.S. security once they dominated their own regions.[259] Because hostile nations now attempt to redraw the international map and malignantly recast regional and worldwide institutions, conventions, and practices, resolute global leadership retains the U.S. postwar policy compass, rejects spheres of influence, and upholds American diplomacy, economic power, and a robust military forward presence. Denying all rivals from securing expansive beachheads from which they can build up their power and ultimately challenge the United States remains a cornerstone of resolute global leadership.[260]

Unlike all the other grand strategies, which contain a coherent internal logic, Trumpism is a particular alternative that vacillates largely on the idiosyncratic preferences of a single individual, Trump. It holds that the United States is a great and exceptional power, but one diminished by its international relationships, which are inherently exploitative and detrimental to U.S. national interests. Consequently, every manifestation of U.S. engagement with the world, beginning with its alliances, continuing through its provision of global collective goods, and ending with its trade, delivers evidence that, as Trump has put it, the United States has been "ripped off for decades by nearly every country on Earth."[261]

Trumpism as a grand strategy promises to redress that abuse. It justifies the president's current policies, for example, to coerce allies into increasing their defense expenditures on the premise that U.S. security guarantees are merely a favor proffered to ungrateful wards; to abandon many international agreements and decry the U.S. provision of global public goods, such as climate change mitigation and development assistance, on the grounds that they are wasteful expenditures that yield no benefits to the United States itself; and to levy extortionate tariffs on U.S. trade partners in order to offset current American trade deficits and alchemize them into permanent surpluses.[262]

Such policies self-evidently suggest that Trumpism cares nothing about legitimacy as an abiding American goal. While some other schools take U.S. preponderance for granted, this one does so most of all. Trump's coarse use of American power corrupts the international system, often heedless of U.S. national interests or the valid rights of others.

Trumpism, in rejecting the liberal international order, permits U.S. adversaries, especially China, to present themselves as the true guardians of a desirable global system.[263] Thus, Trump's disregard for U.S.-created international institutions and alliances carries perils that transcend the loss of legitimacy. While Trumpism undermines international stability, an ascendant China and lesser revisionist powers—Iran, North Korea, and Russia—join forces to subvert the West.[264]

The Trumpist illusion of eliminating those dangers through presidential negotiation has already fallen short, for example, in the case of Ukraine.[265] Because momentous strategic threats persist while the Trump administration undermines U.S. alliances, if a great power conflict occurs, Washington could have to contend with its adversaries largely without the relationships it had long cultivated for that occasion.[266] The heart of the Trumpist theory of security is the conviction that the United States can deal with its adversaries better without its allies than with them.

That approach, telegraphed most clearly by Trump's indiscriminate tariff war, could have been vaguely defensible to some if, for all its legitimacy and security deficiencies, it could amplify the prosperity of the American people. In fact, no imaginable circumstance exists in which unique bilateral trade agreements can enhance U.S. GDP growth, the welfare of the American population, or the resources the United States can mobilize. Trade agreements designed to reduce specific strategic vulnerabilities are sensible. But quixotic efforts at correcting trade deficits with all partners symmetrically, or repatriating manufacturing without regard to its strategic value or efficiency, are simply untenable given every accepted understanding of how modern economies work.

In contrast, the grand strategy of resolute global leadership sets out to preserve the United States' strengths through sustained engagement and leadership in global commerce, including high-standard trade agreements such as the CPTPP, as well as reforms of multilateral regimes such as the World Trade Organization. Further, it envisions increased U.S. defense expenditures to buy back the capacity for dominating power projection, especially along the Asian rimland.[267] Readiness to apply force is essential to successful deterrence, but principally in the face of extraordinary and immediate threats to rigorously defined vital national interests, and never when plausible alternatives are available. Finally, the United States needs to reprise its traditional role of strengthening global order through intense diplomatic engagement with friends and adversaries alike. To all those ends, long-standing U.S. alliances and partnerships are indispensable.

The failures in Afghanistan and Iraq damaged the domestic consensus about the United States' international position, fiscal stability, and military capabilities. Those two wars stoked calls for the United States to fundamentally reduce its global role.[268] Although such sentiments are unsurprising, the alternatives proposed by restraint, American nationalism, and Trumpism would thrust the United States into deadly international competition stripped of much of its armor and its network of essential allies and partners.

To vivify, the Trump administration's national security strategy (NSS), released in early December 2025, is a revolutionary redefinition of the foundations of American foreign policy.[269] With American economic nationalism as the driving engine of the NSS, it condemns the policies of all Trump's predecessors since the end of the Cold War. It stresses American dominance of the Western Hemisphere as the preeminent vital U.S. national interest; focuses on combating illegal immigration and drug trafficking; and pledges to keep the Trump Corollary to the Monroe Doctrine, which will "deny non-Hemispheric competitors the ability to position forces or other threatening capabilities, or to own or control strategically vital assets, in our Hemisphere." It calls for a free and open Indo-Pacific and refers to China as a "near-peer" economy, without directly criticizing Chinese domestic or foreign policies. It bitterly castigates democratic Europe for "censorship of free speech and suppression of political opposition," mass migration, unfair market regulation for U.S. firms, weak defense efforts, and a loss of "civilizational self-confidence." It argues that Europe should take "primary responsibility" for its own defense and that European leaders hold unrealistic expectations about the outcome in Ukraine. It declares its intention to mediate between Russia and NATO in negotiations over Ukraine and other crises, rather than lead the transatlantic alliance in exchanges with Moscow, thus implicitly weakening the U.S. Article 5 commitment. The NSS contains no criticism of Russia.

It reduces the current strategic importance of the Middle East to the United States, while emphasizing economic and business opportunities throughout that region. It urges U.S. allies around the globe to increase their defense spending. It contends that tariffs occupy a central place in efforts to reestablish a fair trade balance for the United States. It insists the United States drop its misguided experiment with hectoring nations into abandoning their traditions and historic forms of government in favor of democratic or other social change. It rejects "the disastrous 'climate change' and 'Net Zero' ideologies." It highlights the dominating role of the sovereign nation-state in the international system and minimizes the contributions of international organizations to global peace and stability.

In short, it embodies the pillars of Trumpist foreign policy.

POLICIES OF THE SIX SCHOOLS OF GRAND STRATEGY

Table 1 indicates how each school would instinctively address current major issues in American foreign policy, with the caveat that immediate circumstances and presidential personalities could well shift those judgments. Even the steadiest presidents sometimes surprise. The chart seeks only to give an overall picture of the substantive thrusts of the alternative grand strategies.

TABLE 1

Instinctive Foreign Policy Positions of Six Schools of American Grand Strategy

	PRIMACY	LIBERAL INTERNATIONALISM	RESTRAINT	AMERICAN NATIONALISM	TRUMPISM	RESOLUTE GLOBAL LEADERSHIP
Contain China	Yes	Yes[a]	No	No	No[b]	Yes
Defend Taiwan	Yes	?[c]	No	No	No[d]	Yes
Initiate a major increase in defense spending	Yes	No	No	No	No	Yes
Continue major military and political support to Ukraine	Yes	Yes	Yes	No	?[e]	Yes
Confirm NATO Article 5	Yes	Yes	Yes	No	?[f]	Yes
Accept Iranian nuclear enrichment	No	Yes	Yes	Yes	Yes	Yes[g]
Use U.S. military force in extremis against the Iranian nuclear program	Yes	No[h]	No	No	?[i]	Yes

a. From the middle of the Obama administration to the end of the Biden administration, the United States lost ground to the rise of Chinese power. See Blackwill and Fontaine, Lost Decade.
b. Although both Secretary of State Marco Rubio and Secretary of Defense Pete Hegseth view China as a regional and global security threat, President Donald Trump follows no perceptible geopolitical approach to China. A case in point is Trump's decision to sell H200 advanced Nvidia chips to China.
c. Despite President Joe Biden asserting four times that the United States would directly defend Taiwan against Chinese aggression, the State Department on each occasion walked back his comments in line with the doctrine of strategic ambiguity. In the event of a Chinese invasion of Taiwan, the daunting prospect of engaging China in a major war over Taiwan 81 miles from China and 6,800 miles from the continental United States would make liberal internationalists hesitate, particularly in the context of progressive influences on this grand strategy school.
d. Consistent with the doctrine of strategic ambiguity, Trump has refused to say whether he would defend Taiwan by military force. And even though the 2025 National Security Strategy has strong language on Taiwan, Trump has persistently pledged to the American people: no more wars.
e. At this writing, it is difficult to anticipate which way Trump's policies will evolve on this subject. He periodically changes his position in a nighttime post only to reverse it a few days later.
f. Ibid.
g. Assuming that the enrichment levels are low (<5% U235), that this level is permanently frozen, and that it can be permanently verified.
h. Although liberal internationalist presidents frequently asserted that all options were on the table regarding the Iranian nuclear program, they put far more emphasis on solving the problem through negotiation than through military action. Most liberal internationalists condemned Trump's attack on Iran's nuclear facilities in June 2025.
i. Trump used military force against three Iranian nuclear sites on June 22, 2025, but only after Israel destroyed Iran's air defenses and severely damaged its nuclear facilities. Without those preconditions, Trump instinctively would have been unlikely to order the U.S. attack because it could have produced U.S. casualties.

Source: Robert D. Blackwill

TABLE 1

Instinctive Foreign Policy Positions of Six Schools of American Grand Strategy (continued)

	PRIMACY	LIBERAL INTERNATIONALISM	RESTRAINT	AMERICAN NATIONALISM	TRUMPISM	RESOLUTE GLOBAL LEADERSHIP
Reform and bolster multilateral trade policy	Yes	?[j]	Yes	No	No	Yes
Impose high tariffs to vitalize the American economy	No	No	No	Yes	Yes	No
Constrain high tech exports to China for national security reasons	Yes	Yes	Yes	No	?[k]	Yes
Promote American values as an important element in U.S. foreign policy	Yes	Yes	No	No	No	Yes
Use force to spread American values	Yes	No	No	No	No	No
Strengthen international institutions	Yes	Yes	Yes	No	No	Yes
Offer the developing world a positive and sympathetic vision of world order	Yes	Yes	Yes	No	No	Yes
Take substantial action to reduce climate change	?[l]	Yes	Yes	No	No	Yes

j. Liberal internationalists abandoned the Trans-Pacific Partnership in 2015 and did not seek to revive it during the Biden administration.
k. At this writing, it is not clear whether Trump will support restrictions through the rest of his term.
l. Primacists rarely address this subject.

Source: Robert D. Blackwill

AMERICA REVIVED

It is clear that the grand strategy of resolute global leadership will be embraced by neither the current president nor the current Republican Party. But the fact remains that there is no irreparable break in the post–World War II order. Most of Trump's dangerous initiatives can, with concerted effort, be reversed. A visionary next president, wedded to constitutional constraints at home and drawing on the enormous inherent power of the United States and its alliances abroad, can, through prudent choices and skillful implementation, restore the United States' preeminent role in shaping a favorable world order, while promoting and defending vital U.S. national interests.

To that end, Trump's successor should reject executive aggrandizement and the current assault on the separation of powers and rule of law. The United States should effectively contend with Chinese power in all of its regional and global dimensions. It should substantially increase the U.S. defense budget and publicly uphold the commitment to NATO's Article 5 obligations and bilateral defense assurances to allies and partners in Asia and the Middle East. While pivoting to the Indo-Pacific, it should expand U.S. naval and airpower capabilities, as well as defensive and offensive space and cyberwarfare assets. It should intensify collective efforts to end the Iranian nuclear weapons program and to contain North Korean proliferation. It should repudiate the U.S. domestic shift toward state capitalism; eliminate indiscriminate global tariffs, especially those on allies and partners; and restore international economic engagement while safeguarding the nation against China's predatory exploitation of trade. It should reinvest in the liberal order by resolving the imbroglio over the World Trade Organization appellate system, joining the CPTPP as well as other international organizations and regimes it exited in recent years, and resuscitating the U.S. Agency for International Development (USAID). It should protect government support for domestic research-and-development institutions and U.S. universities, and their academic freedom. And it should pursue a sensible immigration policy that prioritizes welcoming highly skilled individuals to the United States.

To quote former Secretary of State Madeleine Albright, the United States can again be the "indispensable nation," but only if it behaves like one, which it is entirely capable of doing.[270] Revived U.S. international leadership based on an effective grand strategy is not only possible in 2029, it is imperative.

ENDNOTES

1. See Robert M. Gates, "The Dysfunctional Superpower," *Foreign Affairs*, September 29, 2023, http://foreignaffairs.com/united-states/robert-gates-america-china-russia-dysfunctional-superpower.

2. Robert D. Blackwill and Richard Fontaine, *Lost Decade: The U.S. Pivot to Asia and the Rise of Chinese Power* (New York: Oxford University Press, 2024), 191–223.

3. Graham Allison, Robert D. Blackwill, and Ali Wyne, *Lee Kuan Yew: The Grand Master's Insights on China, the United States, and the World* (Cambridge, MA: MIT Press, 2013), 42.

4. Thierry Balzacq and Ronald R. Krebs, eds., *The Oxford Handbook of Grand Strategy* (Oxford: Oxford University Press, 2021), 2–4; Lukas Milevski, *The Evolution of Modern Grand Strategic Thought* (Oxford: Oxford University Press, 2016), 15–82; B. H. Liddell Hart, *The Decisive Wars of History: A Study in Strategy* (London: G. Bell & Sons, 1929); J. F. C. Fuller, *The Reformation of War* (London: Hutchinson and Co., 1923); Julian S. Corbett, *Some Principles of Maritime Strategy* (London: Longmans, Green, and Co., 1918); and Edward M. Earle, ed., *Makers of Modern Strategy: Military Thought From Machiavelli to Hitler* (Princeton, NJ: Princeton University Press, 1943).

5. B. H. Liddell Hart, *Strategy* (New York: Plume, 1991), 322.

6. F. C. Fuller, *The Generalship of Ulysses S. Grant* (New York: Dodd, Mead and Co., 1929), 5.

7. For further discussion on the meaning of "grand strategy," see: Thierry Balzacq and Ronald R. Krebs, eds., *The Oxford Handbook of Grand Strategy* (Oxford: Oxford University Press, 2021); Hal Brands, *The Promise and Pitfalls of Grand Strategy* (Carlisle, PA: Strategic Studies Institute U.S. Army War College, 2012); Lawrence Freedman, *Strategy: A History* (New York: Oxford University Press, 2013); Paul Kennedy, *The Rise and Fall of the Great Powers: Economic Change and Military Conflict From 1500 to 2000* (New York: Vintage Books, 1987); Henry A. Kissinger, *Diplomacy* (New York: Simon & Schuster, 2011); John Lewis Gaddis, *On Grand Strategy* (New York: Penguin, 2018); Liddell Hart, *Strategy*; John J. Mearsheimer, *The Tragedy of Great Power Politics* (New York: W.W. Norton and Co., 2001); Hans J. Morgenthau, *Politics Among Nations: The Struggle for Power and Peace* (New York: Alfred A. Knopf, 1949); Richard E. Neustadt and Ernest R. May, *Thinking in Time: The Uses of History for Decision Makers* (New York: Free Press, 1986); Thomas C. Schelling, *The Strategy of Conflict* (Cambridge, MA: Harvard University Press, 1981); and Sun Tzu, *The Art of War*, trans. Samuel B. Griffith (New York: Oxford University Press, 1963).

8. Joshua Rovner, *Strategy and Grand Strategy* (London: Routledge, 2025), 10–11. Rovner's framing draws from Barry Posen's famous earlier conceptualization of grand strategy as a "political–military, means–ends chain, a state's theory about how it can best 'cause' security for itself," quoted from Barry R. Posen, *The Sources of Military Doctrine: France, Britain, and Germany Between the World Wars* (Ithaca, NY: Cornell University Press, 1984), 13.

9. Neoconservatism is a specific branch of primacy; at its heart, neoconservatism is the belief that American power is a force for moral progress and that a world shaped by U.S.

leadership—a "benevolent hegemony"—is preferable to any alternative. First articulated in the late Cold War by thinkers such as Irving Kristol and Norman Podhoretz, and later advanced by scholars and commentators such as Robert Kagan, William Kristol, and Paul Wolfowitz, neoconservatism is an extreme offshoot of the grand strategy school of primacy that emphasizes military intervention to promote liberal values. Like other primacists, neoconservatives seek American global and regional military hegemony through substantially increased defense spending and forward military deployment. But they go further and make the global promotion of democracy and human rights a central aim of U.S. foreign policy—pursued through diplomatic and economic pressure, humanitarian interventions, and wars of regime change. Neoconservatives are particularly preoccupied with nuclear proliferation and are more willing than other schools to support preemptive military action to prevent a nuclear breakout. They also reject any drift toward supranational governance and oppose limits on Washington's freedom to act unilaterally as the world's dominant power. See Elliott Abrams, *Security and Sacrifice: Isolation, Intervention, and American Foreign Policy* (Washington, DC: Hudson Institute, 1995); Daniel Bell, *The End of Ideology: On the Exhaustion of Political Ideas in the Fifties* (Cambridge, MA: Harvard University Press, 2000); Peter Berkowitz, "What Neoconservatism Is—and Isn't," *Hoover Digest*, Hoover Institution, October 12, 2008, http://hoover.org/research/what-neoconservatism-and-isnt; Len Colodny and Tom Shachtman, *The Forty Years War: The Rise and Fall of the Neocons, From Nixon to Obama* (New York: HarperCollins, 2009); Douglas J. Feith, *War and Decision: Inside the Pentagon at the Dawn of the War on Terrorism* (New York: HarperCollins, 2008); Janan Ganesh, "The Neocons a Generation On," *Financial Times*, June 28, 2025, http://ft.com/content/07c66858-fe2f-46ee-a67a-765f7d6634c4; Robert Kagan, *Of Paradise and Power: America and Europe in the New World Order* (New York: Vintage, 2004); Robert Kagan, *The Jungle Grows Back* (New York: Knopf Publishing, 2018); Jeane J. Kirkpatrick, *The Withering Away of the Totalitarian State . . . and Other Surprises* (Washington, DC: American Enterprise Institute, 1990); Irving Kristol, *Neo-Conservatism: The Autobiography of an Idea* (New York: Free Press, 1995); Stephen McGlinchey, "Neoconservatism and American Foreign Policy," *E-International Relations*, June 1, 2009, http://e-ir.info/2009/06/01/neo-conservatism-and-american-foreign-policy; Douglas Murray, *Neoconservatism: Why We Need It* (New York: Encounter Books, 2006); Richard Perle and David Frum, *An End to Evil: How to Win the War on Terror* (New York: Ballantine Books, 2004); and Justin Vaïsse, "Why Neoconservatism Still Matters," Policy Paper Number 20, Brookings Institution, May 2010.

10. Although the roots of restraint go back to Renaissance philosopher Niccolò Machiavelli and even Ancient Greek historian Thucydides, modern realism was first formalized in the mid-twentieth century by international relations pioneer Hans Morgenthau and later developed by political scientists such as Kenneth Waltz, Stephen Walt, and John Mearsheimer. Realism is an international relations theory that views states as rational, self-interested actors operating in an anarchic international system. Realists argue that, because no supranational authority exists to enforce rules or guarantee security, states must rely on themselves for survival and pursue their national interest above all else. Moral concerns are not rejected but are always subordinated to the imperatives of security and the national interest. Cooperation through international norms or institutions is possible but only when it aligns with a state's interests or when the cost of disobedience is too high. Realists contend that because states can never be certain of one another's intentions, they must continuously accumulate power to deter threats. Interstate competition and conflict are thus seen not as aberrations but as permanent

features of international politics. Contemporary American academic realists tend to align with the restraint school of grand strategy, but there is nothing inherent in the realist intellectual tradition that ties it to restraint. See Hans J. Morgenthau, *Politics Among Nations: The Struggle for Power and Peace* (New York: Alfred A. Knopf, 1949); Kenneth Waltz, *Theory of International Politics* (Long Grove, IL: Waveland Press, 2010); John J. Mearsheimer, *The Tragedy of Great Power Politics* (New York: W.W. Norton and Co., 2001); Stephen M. Walt, "The Realist Guide to World Peace," *Foreign Policy*, December 23, 2022, http://foreignpolicy.com/2022/12/23/a-realist-guide-to-world-peace; Stephen M. Walt, "The Realist Case for Global Rules," *Foreign Policy*, May 29, 2025, http://foreignpolicy.com/2025/05/29/realism-rules-trump-order-institutions. As for offshore balancing, it was first coined by political scientist Christopher Layne in 1997 as a radical version of the restraint school of grand strategy that emphasizes withdrawing nearly all U.S. military forces from Europe and the Middle East while pursuing the containment of China including, in extremis, by military force to prevent a regional hegemon in the Indo-Pacific in the context of no plausible regional hegemons in either Europe or the Middle East. Stephen Walt and John Mearsheimer, the leading proponents of offshore balancing, argue that "Washington would forgo ambitious efforts to remake other societies and concentrate on what really matters: preserving U.S. dominance in the Western Hemisphere and countering potential hegemons in Europe, Northeast Asia, and the Persian Gulf" (John J. Mearsheimer and Stephen M. Walt, "The Case for Offshore Balancing," *Foreign Affairs*, June 13, 2016, http://foreignaffairs.com/articles/united-states/2016-06-13/case-offshore-balancing). According to offshore balancers, "the United States should turn to regional forces as the first line of defense, letting them uphold the balance of power in their own neighborhood," but "if [local] powers cannot contain a potential hegemon on their own, however, the United States must help get the job done, deploying enough firepower to the region to shift the balance in its favor" (Mearsheimer and Walt, "The Case for Offshore Balancing"). On China, advocates of that position believe that "although Asia contains a number of capable medium-sized powers, such as Japan, South Korea, and India, it will not be easy for them to form an effective balancing coalition. In this case, the United States needs to coordinate this effort and commit its own forces. Buck-passing will not work. Although U.S. military forces will have to be onshore in a number of places in Asia, this policy is still fully consistent with the grand strategy of offshore balancing" (Stephen M. Walt, "The United States Forgot Its Strategy for Winning Cold Wars," *Foreign Policy*, May 5, 2020, http://foreignpolicy.com/2020/05/05/offshore-balancing-cold-war-china-us-grand-strategy). Offshore balancers also argue "the United States should end its military presence [in Europe] and turn NATO over to the Europeans" (Mearsheimer and Walt, "The Case for Offshore Balancing"), and in the Persian Gulf, offshore balancers support "keeping [American] forces out of the region and letting the competing Middle Eastern powers balance each other" (Walt, "The United States Forgot"). See also Christopher Layne, "From Preponderance to Offshore Balancing: America's Future Grand Strategy," *International Security* 22, no. 1 (1997): 86–124, http://jstor.org/stable/2539331.

11. Henry A. Kissinger, *American Foreign Policy: Three Essays* (New York: W.W. Norton & Co., 1974), 74.

12. Graham T. Allison and Robert D. Blackwill, *America's National Interests* (Cambridge, MA: The Commission on America's National Interests, 2000), 13–14.

13. Alexander Hamilton, "Pacificus No. III (6 July, 1793)," July 6, 1793, Founders Online, National Archives, http://founders.archives.gov/documents/Hamilton/01-15-02-0055.

14. Blackwill and Fontaine, *Lost Decade*, 11.

15. Ibid., 12–19.

16. For further discussion on the history of American grand strategy, see: Hal Brands, ed., *The New Makers of Modern Strategy: From the Ancient World to the Digital Age* (Princeton, NJ: Princeton University Press, 2023); Hal Brands and Jeremi Suri, eds., *The Power of the Past: History and Statecraft* (Washington, DC: Brookings Institution Press, 2015); Michael Clarke, *American Grand Strategy and National Security: The Dilemmas of Primacy and Decline From the Founding to Trump* (Cham, Switzerland: Palgrave Macmillan, 2021); Christopher Layne, *The Peace of Illusions: American Grand Strategy From 1940 to the Present* (Ithaca, NY: Cornell University Press, 2006); John Lewis Gaddis, *Strategies of Containment: A Critical Appraisal of Postwar American National Security Policy* (New York: Oxford University Press, 1982); Michael Mandelbaum, *The Four Ages of American Foreign Policy: Weak Power, Great Power, Superpower, Hyperpower* (New York: Oxford University Press, 2022); Walter A. McDougall, *Promised Land, Crusader State: The American Encounter With the World Since 1776* (New York: Mariner Books, 1997); Benjamin Miller and Ziv Rubinovitz, *Grand Strategy From Truman to Trump* (Chicago: University of Chicago Press, 2020); Donald Stoker, *Purpose and Power: U.S. Grand Strategy From the Revolutionary Era to the Present* (Cambridge: Cambridge University Press, 2024); Harry G. Summers Jr., *On Strategy: A Critical Analysis of the Vietnam War* (New York: Presidio Press, 1982); and Robert B. Zoellick, *America in the World: A History of U.S. Diplomacy and Foreign Policy* (New York: Twelve, 2020).

17. "Treaty of Alliance With France (1778)," National Archives and Records Administration, http://archives.gov/milestone-documents/treaty-of-alliance-with-france; and "Treaty of Paris (1783)," National Archives and Records Administration, http://archives.gov/milestone-documents/treaty-of-paris.

18. Gregory J. Dehler, "Neutrality Proclamation," George Washington's Mount Vernon, http://mountvernon.org/library/digitalhistory/digital-encyclopedia/article/neutrality-proclamation.

19. The American nationalism school is often called isolationist. Isolationism certainly has most of the major characteristics of American nationalism but rejects using U.S. military force for any reason outside the Western Hemisphere. See Robert Kagan, *Dangerous Nation: America's Foreign Policy From Its Earliest Days to the Dawn of the Twentieth Century* (New York: Vintage, 2006); Patrick Porter, "Never Alone: Let's Retire the Word 'Isolationism,'" War on the Rocks, May 18, 2016, http://warontherocks.com/2016/05/never-alone-lets-retire-the-word-isolationism; Selig Adler, *The Isolationist Impulse: Its Twentieth-Century Reaction* (New York: Abelard-Schuman, 1957); Condoleezza Rice, "The Perils of Isolationism," *Foreign Affairs*, August 20, 2024, http://foreignaffairs.com/united-states/perils-isolationism-condoleezza-rice.

20. Donald Stoker, *Purpose and Power: U.S. Grand Strategy From the Revolutionary Era to the Present* (Cambridge: Cambridge University Press, 2024), 77–117, 191–224; "The Opening to China Part I: The First Opium War, the United States, and the Treaty of Wangxia, 1839–1844," Milestones: 1830-1860, U.S. Office of the Historian, http://history.state.gov/milestones/1830-1860/china-1; "The United States and the Opening to Japan, 1853," Milestones: 1830-1860, U.S. Office of the Historian, http://history.state.gov/milestones/1830-1860/opening-to-japan; Joe Jackson, *Splendid Liberators: Heroism, Betrayal, Resistance, and the Birth of American Empire* (New York: Farrar, Straus and Giroux, 2025).

21. "The Fourteen Points: Woodrow Wilson and the U.S. Rejection of the Treaty of Versailles," National WWI Museum and Memorial, http://theworldwar.org/learn/peace/fourteen-points.

22. Donald Stoker, *Purpose and Power: U.S. Grand Strategy From the Revolutionary Era to the Present* (Cambridge: Cambridge University Press, 2024), 258–75.

23. "Lend-Lease and Military Aid to the Allies in the Early Years of World War II," Milestones: 1937–1945, U.S. Office of the Historian, http://history.state.gov/milestones/1937-1945/lend-lease; and Andrew Preston, "How FDR Invented National Security," *Foreign Policy*, May 30, 2025, http://foreignpolicy.com/2025/05/30/fdr-roosevelt-national-security-us-foreign-policy-history-quarantine-speech.

24. "Japan, China, the United States and the Road to Pearl Harbor, 1937–41," Milestones: 1937–1945, U.S. Office of the Historian, http://history.state.gov/milestones/1937-1945/pearl-harbor.

25. "NSC-68 and the Korean War," Short History of the Department of State, U.S. Office of the Historian, http://history.state.gov/departmenthistory/short-history/koreanwar.

26. "The Long Telegram," Truman Library Institute, February 22, 2022, http://trumanlibraryinstitute.org/kennan; John Lewis Gaddis, *George F. Kennan: An American Life* (New York: Penguin, 2011); "The Truman Doctrine, 1947," Milestones: 1945-1952, U.S. Office of the Historian, http://history.state.gov/milestones/1945-1952/truman-doctrine; "Marshall Plan, 1948," Milestones: 1945–1952, U.S. Office of the Historian, http://history.state.gov/milestones/1945-1952/marshall-plan; "The Berlin Airlift, 1948-1949," Milestones: 1945–1952, U.S. Office of the Historian, http://history.state.gov/milestones/1945-1952/berlin-airlift; "North Atlantic Treaty Organization (NATO), 1949," Milestones: 1945–1952, U.S. Office of the Historian, http://history.state.gov/milestones/1945-1952/nato; and "NSC-68, 1950," Milestones: 1945–52, U.S. Office of the Historian, http://history.state.gov/milestones/1945-1952/NSC68.

27. H.W. Brands, *America First: Roosevelt vs. Lindbergh in the Shadow of War* (New York: Doubleday, 2024).

28. J. William Fulbright, *The Arrogance of Power* (New York: Random House, 1966).

29. Stephen M. Walt, *The Hell of Good Intentions: America's Foreign Policy Elite and the Decline of U.S. Primacy* (New York: Picador, 2018).

30. "Rapprochement With China, 1972," Milestones: 1969–1976, U.S. Office of the Historian, http://history.state.gov/milestones/1969-1976/rapprochement-china; and "Détente and Arms Control, 1969–1979," Milestones: 1969–1976, U.S. Office of the Historian, http://history.state.gov/milestones/1969-1976/detente.

31. "Carter's Foreign Policy," Short History of the Department of State, U.S. Office of the Historian, http://history.state.gov/departmenthistory/short-history/carter.

32. Hal Brands, *Making the Unipolar Moment: U.S. Foreign Policy and the Rise of the Post–Cold War Order* (Ithaca, NY: Cornell University Press, 2016); and Spencer D. Bakich, *The Gulf War: George H.W. Bush and American Grand Strategy in the Post–Cold War Era* (Lawrence, KS: University Press of Kansas, 2024).

33. Mark Landler and Jane Perlez, "Rare Harmony as China and U.S. Commit to Climate Deal," *New York Times*, September 3, 2016, http://nytimes.com/2016/09/04/world/asia/obama-xi-jinping-china-climate-accord.html; Michael R. Gordon and David

E. Sanger, "Deal Reached on Iran Nuclear Program; Limits on Fuel Would Lessen With Time," *New York Times*, July 14, 2015, http://nytimes.com/2015/07/15/world/ middleeast/iran-nuclear-deal-is-reached-after-long-negotiations.html; Peter Baker and Dan Bilefsky, "Russia and U.S. Sign Nuclear Arms Reduction Pact," *New York Times*, April 8, 2010, http://nytimes.com/2010/04/09/world/europe/09prexy.html; Kevin Granville, "What Is TPP? Behind the Trade Deal That Died," *New York Times*, January 23, 2017, http://nytimes.com/interactive/2016/business/tpp-explained-what- is-trans-pacific-partnership.html; and "FACT SHEET: The Obama Administration's Record on the Trade Enforcement," Press Office, Obama White House, January 12, 2017, http://obamawhitehouse.archives.gov/the-press-office/2017/01/12/fact-sheet-obama- administrations-record-trade-enforcement.

34. Mark Landler, "Trump Abandons Iran Nuclear Deal He Long Scorned," *New York Times*, May 8, 2018, http://nytimes.com/2018/05/08/world/middleeast/trump-iran-nuclear-deal. html; "President Trump Announces U.S. Withdrawal From the Paris Climate Accord," Trump White House, June 1, 2017, http://trumpwhitehouse.archives.gov/articles/ president-trump-announces-u-s-withdrawal-paris-climate-accord; Katie Rogers and Apoorva Mandavilli, "Trump Administration Signals Formal Withdrawal From W.H.O." *New York Times*, July 7, 2020, http://nytimes.com/2020/07/07/us/politics/coronavirus- trump-who.html; David E. Sanger, "Trump Will Withdraw From Open Skies Arms Control Treaty," *New York Times*, May 21, 2020, http://nytimes.com/2020/05/21/us/ politics/trump-open-skies-treaty-arms-control.html; Zachary Cohen, Michelle Kosinski, and Barbara Starr, "Trump's Barrage of Attacks 'Beyond Belief,' Reeling NATO Diplomats Say," CNN, July 12, 2018, http://cnn.com/2018/07/11/politics/trump-nato- diplomats-reaction; and Ana Swanson, "Trump's Trade War With China Is Officially Underway," *New York Times*, July 5, 2018, http://nytimes.com/2018/07/05/business/china- us-trade-war-trump-tariffs.html.

35. Charles A. Kupchan, "Biden's Legacy: Major Accomplishments but Unfinished Business," Council on Foreign Relations, July 25, 2024, http://cfr.org/expert-brief/bidens-legacy- major-accomplishments-unfinished-business.

36. The pillars and critiques for primacy and the ensuing pillars and critiques for the other four schools of U.S. grand strategy are all drawn from specific commentary on the subject. For further discussion on the grand strategy of primacy, see: Brands, *Making the Unipolar Moment*; Hal Brands, "Choosing Primacy: U.S. Strategy and the Global Order at the Dawn of the Post-Cold War Era," *Texas National Security Review* 1, no. 2 (February 2018): 8–33, http://doi.org/10.15781/T2VH5D166; Zbigniew Brzezinski, *The Grand Chessboard: American Primacy and Its Geostrategic Imperatives* (New York: Basic Books, 1997); Eliot A. Cohen, *The Big Stick: The Limits of Soft Power and the Necessity of Military Force* (New York: Basic Books, 2016); Daniel Drezner, "Military Primacy Doesn't Pay (Nearly as Much as You Think)," *International Security* 38, no. 1 (Summer 2013): 52–79, http://jstor.org/ stable/24480569; Richard Haass, "Pondering Primacy," *Georgetown Journal of International Affairs* 4, no. 2 (Summer/Fall 2003): 91–98, http://jstor.org/stable/43133529; Stanley Hoffmann, *Primacy or World Order: American Foreign Policy Since the Cold War* (New York: McGraw-Hill, 1978); Samuel P. Huntington, "Why International Primacy Matters," *International Security* 17, no. 4 (Spring 1993): 68–83, http://jstor.org/stable/2539022; Joseph S. Nye Jr., *The Paradox of American Power: Why the World's Only Superpower Can't Go It Alone* (Oxford: Oxford University Press, 2002); Bradley A. Thayer, "In Defense of Primacy," *National Interest*, no. 86 (November–December 2006): 32–37, http://nationalinterest.org/ legacy/in-defense-of-primacy-1300; and Walt, *The Hell of Good Intentions*.

37. Brands, "Choosing Primacy."

38. Stephen G. Brooks, G. John Ikenberry, and William C. Wohlforth, "Don't Come Home, America: The Case Against Retrenchment," *International Security* 37, no. 3 (2013): 7–51, http://doi.org/10.1162/ISEC_a_00107.

39. Patrick Porter, "Why America's Grand Strategy Has Not Changed: Power, Habit, and the U.S. Foreign Policy Establishment," *International Security* 42, no. 4 (2018): 9–46, http://doi.org/10.1162/isec_a_00311.

40. Bret Stephens, *America in Retreat: The New Isolationism and the Coming Global Disorder* (New York: Sentinel, 2014), 143.

41. George P. Shultz, "The Ten Commandments of Foreign Policy," *Hoover Digest*, Hoover Institution, April 30, 1997, http://hoover.org/research/ten-commandments-foreign-policy.

42. Max Bergmann, "How America Blew Its Unipolar Moment," *Foreign Policy*, May 26, 2025, http://foreignpolicy.com/2025/05/26/how-america-blew-its-unipolar-moment.

43. Barry R. Posen, *Restraint: A New Foundation for U.S. Grand Strategy* (Ithaca, NY: Cornell University Press, 2014), 35–50; and Dan Caldwell, "The Case for a Restrained Republican Foreign Policy," *Foreign Affairs*, March 22, 2023, http://foreignaffairs.com/united-states/foreign-policy-republican-american-power.

44. J. William Fulbright, *The Arrogance of Power* (New York: Random House, 1966), 3–4.

45. For further discussion on the grand strategy of liberal internationalism, see James M. Lindsay, "A New U.S. Grand Strategy: The Case for Liberal Internationalism, With G. John Ikenberry," *The President's Inbox* podcast, Council on Foreign Relations, May 7, 2024, http://cfr.org/podcasts/new-us-grand-strategy-case-liberal-internationalism-g-john-ikenberry; Bryan H. Druzin, "How to Destroy the Liberal International Order," *Duke Journal of Comparative and International Law* 34, no. 1 (2024): 1–37, http://scholarship.law.duke.edu/djcil/vol34/iss1/1; Colin Dueck, "Hegemony on the Cheap: Liberal Internationalism From Wilson to Bush," *World Policy Journal* 20, no. 4 (Winter 2003/2004): 1–11, http://jstor.org/stable/40209884; Charles L. Glaser, "A Flawed Framework: Why the Liberal International Order Concept Is Misguided," *International Security* 43, no. 4 (2019): 51–87, http://doi.org/10.1162/isec_a_00343; Stanley Hoffmann, "The Crisis of Liberal Internationalism," *Foreign Policy*, no. 98 (Spring 1995): 159–177, http://doi.org/10.2307/1148964; G. John Ikenberry, "Liberal Internationalism 3.0: America and the Dilemmas of Liberal World Order," *Perspectives on Politics* 7, no. 1 (2009): 71–87, http://doi.org/10.1017/S1537592709090112; G. John Ikenberry, "The Future of the Liberal World Order: Internationalism After America," *Foreign Affairs* 90, no. 3 (May–June 2011): 56–68, http://foreignaffairs.com/future-liberal-world-order; John J. Mearsheimer, *The Great Delusion: Liberal Dreams and International Realities* (New Haven: Yale University Press, 2018); John J. Mearsheimer, "The False Promise of International Institutions," *International Security* 19, no. 3 (Winter 1994/1995): 5–49, http://doi.org/10.2307/2539078; John M. Owen IV, "Liberal Internationalism, Then and Now," in *The Ecology of Nations: American Democracy in a Fragile World Order* (New Haven: Yale University Press, 2023), 103–141; Anne-Marie Slaughter, "How America Can Succeed in a Multialigned World," *Foreign Affairs*, October 30, 2024, http://foreignaffairs.com/united-states/how-america-can-succeed-multialigned-world; and Van Jackson, *Grand Strategies of the Left: The Foreign Policy of Progressive Worldmaking* (Cambridge: Cambridge University Press, 2023).

46. G. John Ikenberry, *Liberal Leviathan: The Origins, Crisis, and Transformation of the American World Order* (Princeton, NJ: Princeton University Press, 2011); Slaughter, "How America Can Succeed in a Multialigned World"; and Walt, "The Realist Case for Global Rules."

47. G. John Ikenberry, *A World Safe for Democracy: Liberal Internationalism and the Crises of Global Order* (New Haven: Yale University Press, 2020); Anne-Marie Slaughter, *The Idea That Is America: Keeping Faith With Our Values in a Dangerous World* (New York: Basic Books, 2007); and Sean Lynn-Jones, "Why the United States Should Spread Democracy," Belfer Center for Science and International Affairs, Harvard Kennedy School, March 1998, http://belfercenter.org/publication/why-united-states-should-spread-democracy.

48. John F. Kennedy, "Speech by Senator John F. Kennedy, Convention Hall, Philadelphia, PA," American Presidency Project, October 31, 1960, http://presidency.ucsb.edu/node/274847.

49. Ikenberry, *Liberal Leviathan.*

50. Vali Nasr, *The Dispensable Nation: American Foreign Policy in Retreat* (New York: Doubleday, 2013).

51. Slaughter, "How America Can Succeed in a Multialigned World."

52. Josh Rogin, "The Obama Administration Is Failing to Stop China's Pacific Aggression," *Washington Post*, June 24, 2016, http://washingtonpost.com/opinions/global-opinions/the-obama-administration-is-failing-to-stop-chinas-pacific-aggression/2016/06/23/fce65f98-396c-11e6-8f7c-d4c723a2becb_story.html; Lindsay Maizland and Clara Fong, "Why China-Taiwan Relations Are So Tense," Council on Foreign Relations, Last Updated March 19, 2025, http://cfr.org/backgrounder/china-taiwan-relations-tension-us-policy-trump#chapter-title-0-4; Adrian Karatnycky, "The Long, Destructive Shadow of Obama's Russia Doctrine," *Foreign Policy*, July 11, 2023, http://foreignpolicy.com/2023/07/11/obama-russia-ukraine-war-putin-2014-crimea-georgia-biden; Elliot Ackerman, "The Biden Administration's Slow Yes Has Doomed Ukraine," *Time*, December 18, 2023, http://time.com/6548816/ukraine-biden-administration-military-aid; Dennis Ross, "How Obama Created a Mideast Vacuum," Washington Institute for Near East Policy, January 10, 2016, http://washingtoninstitute.org/policy-analysis/how-obama-created-mideast-vacuum; Kali Robinson, "What Is The Iran Nuclear Deal?," Council on Foreign Relations, October 27, 2023, http://cfr.org/backgrounder/what-iran-nuclear-deal#chapter-title-0-5; "Biden Protects Iran's Nuclear Program," *Wall Street Journal*, October 2, 2024, http://wsj.com/opinion/iran-israel-strikes-benjamin-netanyahu-joe-biden-8e6d044d; Michael Crowley, "Obama's 'Red Line' Haunts Clinton, Trump," *Politico*, October 11, 2016, http://politico.com/story/2016/09/obama-clinton-syria-red-line-228585; Tara Copp, "WATCH: Top Former Generals Say Planning Failures of Biden Administration Drove Chaotic Fall of Kabul," *PBS News Hour*, March 19, 2024, http://pbs.org/newshour/politics/watch-top-former-generals-say-planning-failures-of-biden-administration-drove-chaotic-fall-of-kabul; Dan Merica and Eric Bradner, "Hillary Clinton Comes Out Against TPP Trade Deal," CNN, October 7, 2015, http://cnn.com/2015/10/07/politics/hillary-clinton-opposes-tpp; and Anthony Zurcher, "'Trump Was Right'—John Kerry Says Democrats Allowed Migrant 'Siege' of U.S. Border," BBC News, July 10, 2025, http://bbc.com/news/articles/cr4wk52rwqpo.

53. Emma Ashford, "America Can't Escape the Multipolar Order," *The Foreign Affairs Interview Podcast, Foreign Affairs*, December 4, 2025, http://foreignaffairs.com/podcasts/america-cant-escape-multipolar-order; Emma Ashford, *First Among Equals: U.S. Foreign*

Policy in a Multipolar World (New Haven, CT: Yale University Press, 2025); Christopher Preble, *A Credible Grand Strategy: The Urgent Need to Set Priorities* (Washington, DC: Stimson Center, 2024), http://stimson.org/2024/a-credible-grand-strategy-the-urgent-need-to-set-priorities; Rebecca Lissner and Mira Rapp-Hooper, "Absent at the Creation?," *Foreign Affairs*, June 24, 2025, http://foreignaffairs.com/united-states/absent-creation-rebecca-lissner; Arancha Gonzalez Laya, "The Search for a New International Order in a Fractured World," *Horizons*, no. 23 (Spring 2023): 154–63; and Gordon Brown, "The 'New World Order' of the Past 35 Years Is Being Demolished Before Our Eyes. This Is How We Must Proceed," *The Guardian*, April 12, 2025, http://theguardian.com/commentisfree/2025/apr/12/new-world-order-conflict-era-multilateralism.

54. Ibid.

55. "GDP (current US$)—United States, World," World Bank Open Data, accessed July 24, 2025, http://data.worldbank.org/indicator/NY.GDP.MKTP.CD?locations=US-1W.

56. Aaron Mehta and Valerie Insinna, "$895.2 Billion Compromise NDAA Released, Sliding Under Fiscal Responsibility Act Cap Levels," *Breaking Defense*, December 7, 2024, http://breakingdefense.com/2024/12/895-2-billion-compromise-ndaa-released-sliding-under-fiscal-responsibility-act-cap-levels.

57. Arturo McFields, "Never Mind What You Heard—the BRICS Summit Failed Before It Began," *The Hill*, July 5, 2025, http://thehill.com/opinion/international/5384097-the-brics-summit-failed-before-it-began.

58. For further discussion on the grand strategy of restraint, see: "A New U.S. Grand Strategy: The Case for a Realist Foreign Policy, With Stephen Walt," *The President's Inbox* podcast, Council on Foreign Relations, August 26, 2025, http://cfr.org/podcasts/tpi/new-us-grand-strategy-case-realist-foreign-policy-stephen-walt; Hal Brands, *The Limits of Offshore Balancing* (Carlisle, PA: U.S. Army War College Press, 2015); Brooks, Ikenberry, and Wohlforth, "Don't Come Home, America: The Case Against Retrenchment," *International Security* 37, no. 3 (2013): 7–51, http://doi.org/10.1162/ISEC_a_00107; Dan Caldwell, "The Case for a Restrained Republican Foreign Policy," *Foreign Affairs*, March 22, 2023, http://foreignaffairs.com/united-states/foreign-policy-republican-american-power; Eugene Gholz, Daryl G. Press, and Harvey M. Sapolsky, "Come Home, America: The Strategy of Restraint in the Face of Temptation," *International Security* 21, no. 4 (1997): 5–48, http://doi.org/10.2307/2539282; Christopher Layne, "From Preponderance to Offshore Balancing: America's Future Grand Strategy," *International Security* 22, no. 1 (1997): 86–124, http://jstor.org/stable/2539331; Mearsheimer and Walt, "The Case for Offshore Balancing"; Posen, *Restraint*; Barry R. Posen and Andrew L. Ross, "Competing Visions for U.S. Grand Strategy," *International Security* 21, no. 3 (Winter 1996–7): 5–53, http://doi.org/10.2307/2539272; Christopher A. Preble, *The Power Problem: How American Military Dominance Makes Us Less Safe, Less Prosperous, and Less Free* (Ithaca, NY: Cornell University Press, 2009); Miranda Priebe, Kristen Gunness, Karl P. Mueller, and Zachary Burdette, *The Limits of Restraint: The Military Implications of a Restrained U.S. Grand Strategy in the Asia-Pacific* (Santa Monica, CA: RAND Corporation, 2022), http://rand.org/pubs/research_reports/RRA739-4.html; Miranda Priebe, John Schuessler, Bryan Rooney, and Jasen Castillo, "Competing Visions of Restraint," *International Security* 49, no. 2 (2024): 135–69, http://doi.org/10.1162/isec_a_00498; and C. William Walldorf Jr. and Andrew Yeo, "Domestic Hurdles to a Grand Strategy of Restraint," *Washington Quarterly* 42, no. 4 (2019): 43–56, http://doi.org/10.1080/0163660X.2019.1693107.

59. John Quincy Adams, "An Address Delivered at the Request of a Committee of the Citizens of Washington; on the Occasion of Reading the Declaration of Independence, on the Fourth of July, 1821," speech, Washington, DC, July 4, 1821, Reproduced by the John Quincy Adams Society, http://jqas.org/jqas-monsters-to-destroy-speech-full-text.

60. J. William Fulbright, *The Arrogance of Power* (New York: Random House, 1966); Walt, *The Hell of Good Intentions*; and Stephen Wertheim, "America Made a Catastrophic Mistake With the Iraq War. Is It About to Repeat It in Iran?" *The Guardian*, June 20, 2025, http://theguardian.com/commentisfree/2025/jun/20/america-made-a-catastrophic-mistake-with-the-iraq-war-is-it-about-to-repeat-it-in-iran.

61. Hal Brands, Peter D. Feaver, John J. Mearsheimer, and Stephen M. Walt, "Should American Retrench?," *Foreign Affairs* 95, no. 6 (November/December 2016): 164–71, http://foreignaffairs.com/united-states/should-america-retrench.

62. Frank G. Hoffman, "Retreating Ashore: The Flaws of Offshore Balancing," *Geopoliticus*, Foreign Policy Research Institute, July 5, 2016, http://fpri.org/2016/07/retreating-ashore-flaws-offshore-balancing.

63. Ibid.

64. Winston S. Churchill, "The Gift of a Common Tongue," speech, Harvard University, Cambridge, MA, September 6, 1943, reproduced by the International Churchill Society, http://winstonchurchill.org/resources/speeches/1941-1945-war-leader/the-gift-of-a-common-tongue.

65. For further discussion on the grand strategy of American nationalism, see: Andrew J. Bacevich, "Saving 'America First': What Responsible Nationalism Looks Like," *Foreign Affairs* 96, no. 5 (September/October 2017): 57–67, http://foreignaffairs.com/united-states/saving-america-first; Antony J. Blinken and Robert Kagan, "'America First' Is Only Making the World Worse. Here's a Better Approach," Brookings Institution, January 4, 2019, http://brookings.edu/articles/america-first-is-only-making-the-world-worse-heres-a-better-approach; Hal Brands, "U.S. Grand Strategy in an Age of Nationalism: Fortress America and Its Alternatives," *Washington Quarterly* 40, no. 1 (2017): 73–94, http://doi.org/10.1080/0163660X.2017.1302740; Michael Brenes and Van Jackson, "Trump and the New Age of Nationalism," *Foreign Affairs*, January 28, 2025, http://foreignaffairs.com/united-states/trump-and-new-age-nationalism; Krishnadev Calamur, "A Short History of 'America First,'" *The Atlantic*, January 21, 2017, http://theatlantic.com/politics/archive/2017/01/trump-america-first/514037; Jonathan Kirshner, "Trump's 'America First' Is Not Realism," *Foreign Affairs*, January 22, 2025, http://foreignaffairs.com/united-states/trumps-america-first-not-realism; Michael Lind, "The Case for American Nationalism," *National Interest*, no. 131 (May–June 2014): 9–20, http://jstor.org/stable/44153287; Paul T. McCartney, "American Nationalism and U.S. Foreign Policy From September 11 to the Iraq War," *Political Science Quarterly* 119, no. 3 (Fall 2004): 399–423, http://doi.org/10.2307/20202389; Eric Rauchway, "How 'America First' Got Its Nationalistic Edge," *The Atlantic*, May 6, 2016, http://theatlantic.com/politics/archive/2016/05/william-randolph-hearst-gave-america-first-its-nationalist-edge/481497; Walter Russell Mead, "The Jacksonian Tradition and American Foreign Policy," *National Interest*, no. 58 (Winter 1999/2000): 5–29, http://jstor.org/stable/42897216; and Walter Russell Mead, "The Jacksonian Revolt: American Populism and the Liberal Order," *Foreign Affairs* 96, no. 2 (March–April 2017): 2–7, http://foreignaffairs.com/north-america/jacksonian-revolt.

66. Brands, "U.S. Grand Strategy in an Age of Nationalism."

67. Lind, "The Case for American Nationalism."

68. Marjorie Taylor Greene (@RepMTG), "Amendment Announcement for Defense Appropriations Funding Bill With a Sprinkle of a Slight Rant and Sarcasm Delivered on a Bed of Raw Truth . . ," July 8, 2025, 6:16 p.m., http://x.com/RepMTG/status/1942709412088390072; Eve Sampson, "J.D. Vance's Opposition to U.S. Support for Ukraine: In His Own Words," *New York Times*, July 15, 2024, http://nytimes.com/2024/07/15/world/europe/ukraine-jd-vance.html; Sonam Sheth, "Tucker Carlson and Steve Bannon Lead MAGA Resistance to Iran War," *Newsweek*, June 16, 2025, http://newsweek.com/tucker-carlson-steve-bannon-maga-trump-iran-israel-war-2086346; and Alex Nitzberg, "Elon Musk Agrees With Ron Paul's Call to 'ELIMINATE Foreign Aid,'" Fox News, December 9, 2024, http://foxnews.com/politics/elon-musk-agrees-ron-pauls-call-eliminate-foreign-aid.

69. Paul McLeary and Daniel Lippman, "Pentagon Plan Prioritizes Homeland Over China Threat," *Politico*, September 5, 2025, http://politico.com/news/2025/09/05/pentagon-national-defense-strategy-china-homeland-western-hemisphere-00546310?s=09&t=1aKEx-wQTa0fHiM68n_I7Q; Graig Graziosi, "Tucker Carlson Sparks Backlash After Asking for U.S. Troops to Liberate Canada," *The Independent*, January 27, 2023, http://independent.co.uk/news/world/americas/us-politics/tucker-carlson-liberate-canada-backlash-b2270891.html; Chuck DeVore, "Why Trump Is Right to Revitalize the Monroe Doctrine," Fox News, April 18, 2025, http://foxnews.com/opinion/why-trump-right-revitalize-monroe-doctrine; and Clarissa-Jan Lim, "Elon Musk Can't Stop Fearmongering on Immigration," MSNBC, March 5, 2024, http://msnbc.com/top-stories/latest/elon-musk-conspiracy-theory-immigration-terror-rcna141827.

70. Henry Cabot Lodge, "League of Nations," speech, Washington, DC, August 12, 1919, recorded in Nation's Forum Collection, and A.F.R. Lawrence Collection, Bridgeport, CT, made by the Columbia Graphophone Manufacturing Company, http://loc.gov/item/2004650542.

71. Joe Hasell, Bertha Rohenkohl, Pablo Arriagada, Esteban Ortiz-Ospina, and Max Roser, "Poverty," Our World in Data, 2022, http://ourworldindata.org/poverty; Saloni Dattani, Lucas Rodés-Guirao, Hannah Ritchie, Esteban Ortiz-Ospina, and Max Roser, "Life Expectancy," Our World in Data, 2023, http://ourworldindata.org/life-expectancy; and Max Roser, "Child Mortality: an Everyday Tragedy of Enormous Scale That We Can Make Progress Against," Our World in Data, 2021, http://ourworldindata.org/child-mortality-big-problem-in-brief.

72. John Lewis Gaddis, "The Long Peace: Elements of Stability in the Postwar International System." *International Security* 10, no. 4 (Spring 1986): 99–142, http://jstor.org/stable/2538951; and Editorial Board, "Tulsi Gabbard's Nuclear Strategy," *Wall Street Journal*, June 13, 2025, http://wsj.com/opinion/tulsi-gabbard-nuclear-strategy-atomic-bomb-donald-trump-russia-iran-caa59264.

73. Benjamin Miller and Ziv Rubinovitz, *Grand Strategy From Truman to Trump* (Chicago: University of Chicago Press, 2020), 242; and Antony J. Blinken and Robert Kagan, "'America First' Is Only Making the World Worse. Here's a Better Approach," Brookings Institution, January 4, 2019, http://brookings.edu/articles/america-first-is-only-making-the-world-worse-heres-a-better-approach.

74. Tobias Burns, "What Tariffs Could Mean for U.S. Workers, Consumers and the Economy," *The Hill*, April 3, 2025, http://thehill.com/business/5230405-trump-tariffs-economic-effects.

75. For further discussion on the grand strategy of Trumpism, see: Michael Anton, "The Trump Doctrine," *Foreign Policy*, April 20, 2019, http://foreignpolicy.com/2019/04/20/the-trump-doctrine-big-think-america-first-nationalism; Hal Brands, *American Grand Strategy in the Age of Trump* (Washington, DC: Brookings Institution Press, 2018); Hal Brands, "An 'America First' World," *Foreign Affairs*, May 27, 2024, http://foreignaffairs.com/united-states/america-first-world-trump; Michael Clarke and Anthony Ricketts, "Donald Trump and American Foreign Policy: The Return of the Jacksonian Tradition," *Comparative Strategy* 36, no. 4 (2017): 366–79, http://doi.org/10.1080/01495933.2017.1361210; James Curran, "'Americanism, Not Globalism': President Trump and the American Mission," Lowy Institute for International Policy, July 3, 2018, http://jstor.org/stable/resrep19793; Ross Douthat, "Trump and Vance Are Stripping Away Foreign Policy Illusions," *New York Times*, March 1, 2025, http://nytimes.com/2025/03/01/opinion/trump-vance-zelensky.html; Editorial Board, "Trump's Old World Order," *Wall Street Journal*, March 2, 2025, http://wsj.com/opinion/trumps-brave-old-world-foreign-policy-ukraine-blow-up-china-russia-trade-allies-7e32b02a; Robert C. O'Brien, "The Case for Trump's Second-Term Foreign Policy," *Foreign Affairs*, November 5, 2025, http://foreignaffairs.com/united-states/case-trumps-second-term-foreign-policy; Francis P. Sempa, "Trump's Foreign Policy Abandons Ideology for the Balance of Power," RealClearDefense, February 28, 2025, http://realcleardefense.com/articles/2025/02/28/trumps_foreign_policy_abandons_ideology_for_the_balance_of_power_1094506.html; Jacob Shively, *Make America First Again: Grand Strategy Analysis and the Trump Administration* (Amherst, NY: Cambria Press, 2020); "Pillar VI: Deliver Peace Through Strength and American Leadership," in *America First Agenda: Guide to the Issues*, Scott Toland, Aaron Hedlund, and Steve Smith, eds., America First Policy Institute, (Washington, DC: America First Policy Institute), http://agenda.americafirstpolicy.com/strengthen-leadership; Trump White House, *National Security Strategy of the United States of America*, November 2025, http://whitehouse.gov/wp-content/uploads/2025/12/2025-National-Security-Strategy.pdf; Stephen M. Walt, "Donald Trump Will Never Be a Restrainer," *Foreign Policy*, September 30, 2025, http://foreignpolicy.com/2025/09/30/donald-trump-foreign-policy-restrainer-realist-war-defense-diplomacy; Stephen Wertheim, "Trump Is a Situational Man in a Structural Bind," *New York Times*, July 22, 2025, http://nytimes.com/2025/07/22/opinion/trump-america-foreign-policy.html; and Fareed Zakaria, "Trump Is Reorienting America's Moral Compass," *Washington Post*, March 2, 2025, http://washingtonpost.com/opinions/2025/03/02/trump-zelensky-vance-freedom-policy. Trump rejects three of the five vital national interests outlined in the introduction. First, Trump has repeatedly signaled a lack of commitment to defend allies, undermining NATO's Article 5 by stating, "If you're not gonna pay, we're not gonna defend" (Gabe Whisnant and Andrew Stanton, "Donald Trump Draws Red Line for Defending NATO Allies," *Newsweek*, March 6, 2025, http://newsweek.com/trump-weighs-overhaul-nato-commitments-based-defense-spending-report-2040708). Second, Trump regularly weakens domestic U.S. robustness by attacking constitutional checks and balances; he has degraded American international influence through his cuts to USAID; and he has heaped scorn on the U.S. alliance system, particularly NATO (Adam Liptak, "Trump's Actions Have Created a Constitutional Crisis, Scholars Say," *New York Times*, February 10, 2025, http://nytimes.com/2025/02/10/us/politics/trump-constitutional-crisis.html; Karoun Demirjian, Stephanie Nolen, Michael Crowley, and Elizabeth Dias, "Final Cuts Will Eliminate U.S. Aid Agency in All but Name," *New York Times*, March 28, 2025, http://nytimes.com/2025/03/28/us/politics/usaid-trump-doge-cuts.html; and Hugh Cameron, "Five Things Donald Trump Has Said About NATO,"

Newsweek, November 13, 2024, http://newsweek.com/five-things-donald-trump-said-about-nato-1985307). And third, Trump rejects the major international systems: he insists that "tariffs are the greatest thing ever invented," injuring the global trade regime; he declares his disinterest in preserving the global commons as early as 1987: "The world is laughing at American politicians as we protect ships we don't own, carrying oil we don't need, destined for allies who won't help"; and he denigrates the United Nations, saying, "When do you see the United Nations solving problems? They don't. They cause problems" (Kelly Hayes, "Explain Tariffs to Me: What Are They? How Do They Work?" Fox 10 Phoenix, March 4, 2025, http://fox10phoenix.com/news/explain-tariffs-me-what-they-how-do-work; Michael Kruse, "The True Story of Donald Trump's First Campaign Speech—in 1987," *Politico*, February 5, 2016, http://politico.com/magazine/story/2016/02/donald-trump-first-campaign-speech-new-hampshire-1987-213595; and John Wagner, "Trump Re-Ups Criticism of United Nations, Saying It's Causing Problems, Not Solving Them," *Washington Post*, December 28, 2016, http://washingtonpost.com/news/post-politics/wp/2016/12/28/trump-re-ups-criticism-of-united-nations-saying-its-causing-problems-not-solving-them). Trump's second-term foreign policy is unusually personalized: Trump conducts much of his approach via his personal cell phone and takes direct calls from leaders such as Emmanuel Macron, Keir Starmer, and Mohammed bin Salman outside secure channels and often without staff, creating obvious security and miscommunication risks (Ashley Parker and Michael Scherer, "The Secret History of Trump's Private Cellphone," *The Atlantic*, June 2, 2025, http://theatlantic.com/politics/archive/2025/06/trump-private-cellphone-china-hackers/683006; and Sam Sabin, "Trump Might Be the Most Accessible President Ever—for Spies or Scammers," Axios, June 8, 2025, http://axios.com/2025/06/08/donald-trump-cell-phone-security-hackers). Leaders have learned that personal flattery moves Trump's policy: NATO's Mark Rutte texted Trump that "Europe is going to pay in a BIG way. . . . You will achieve something NO American president in decades could get done," and Rutte compared Trump to a "daddy." At the June 2025 NATO Summit, Trump subsequently proved more cooperative with NATO and Ukraine (Will Weissert, "'Dear Donald.' Trump Posts Fawning Private Text From NATO Chief on Social Media," Associated Press, June 24, 2025, http://apnews.com/article/trump-rutte-text-message-nato-signal-6263810ac3ca77a5bf7366499f51c772; Brian Melley, "Zelenskyy Deploys Gratitude Diplomacy in Second White House Meeting With Trump," Associated Press, August 19, 2025, http://apnews.com/article/thank-you-diplomacy-trump-zelenskyy-russia-ukraine-d2f4ce2a0a27f81dba8ea07f5fb1bfd3; and Laurie Kellman, "Trump Management 101: World Leaders Adapt to His Erratic Diplomacy With Flattery and Patience," Associated Press, June 27, 2025, http://apnews.com/article/trump-nato-rutte-flattery-daddy-iran-e7ee4dacb4febf14e3911f376638daaa). Personal grievances also drive decisions, most starkly when Trump paused U.S. military aid to Ukraine after an Oval Office blowup with Ukrainian President Volodymyr Zelenskyy (Erica L. Green et al., "Trump Suspends Military Aid to Ukraine After Oval Office Blowup," *New York Times*, March 3, 2025, Last Updated March 5, 2025, http://nytimes.com/2025/03/03/us/politics/trump-ukraine-military-aid.html).

76. Trump has placed the greatest priority in his foreign policy on redressing U.S. trade imbalances through tariffs and trade deals. He has leveraged international crises to secure economic gains for the United States, as seen in the rare-earths deal with Ukraine, the potential mining rights agreement with Democratic Republic of Congo, and his pursuit of Greenland's minerals (Atlantic Council Experts, "Experts React: How the World Is Responding to Trump's 'Liberation Day' Tariffs," *New Atlanticist*, Atlantic Council, April 4, 2025, http://atlanticcouncil.org/blogs/new-atlanticist/experts-react/experts-react-

how-the-world-is-responding-to-trumps-liberation-day-tariffs; Lingling Wei, "Trump Is Shifting to Dealmaking Mode on China," *Wall Street Journal*, July 24, 2025, http://wsj.com/economy/trade/trump-china-trade-dealmaking-995d7717; Paul Kirby, James FitzGerald, and Tom Geoghegan, "Seven Takeaways From U.S.-Ukraine Resources Deal," BBC News, May 1, 2025, http://bbc.com/news/articles/c5yg456mzn8o; Nicolas Niarchos, "Just How Badly Does Donald Trump Want Access to Critical Minerals?" *New Yorker*, April 15, 2025, http://newyorker.com/news/the-lede/just-how-badly-does-donald-trump-want-access-to-critical-minerals; Ido Vock, "Why Does Trump Want Greenland and What Do Its People Think?" BBC News, March 24, 2025, http://bbc.com/news/articles/c74x4m71pmjo; and Demetri Sevastopulo, "U.S. Halts Plans to Sanction Chinese Spy Agency," *Financial Times*, December 3, 2025, http://ft.com/content/61016803-baf5-4be5-8350-e0cc5ca4ab26). Trade was the centerpiece of Trump's October 2025 tour of Asia as he secured trade deals with Cambodia, China, Japan, Malaysia, South Korea, Thailand, and Vietnam (Bart Jansen, "Trade Deals, Pageantry and Nukes: 7 Takeaways From Trump's Trip to Asia," *USA Today*, October 30, 2025, http://usatoday.com/story/news/politics/2025/10/30/trump-asia-trip-trade-deals-china-south-korea/86947760007).

77.   Trump's long-standing opposition to faraway U.S. military interventions has been a consistent theme throughout his political career. In 2018, he tweeted: "Does the USA want to be the Policeman of the Middle East, getting NOTHING but spending precious lives and trillions of dollars protecting others who, in almost all cases, do not appreciate what we are doing? Do we want to be there forever? Time for others to finally fight" (Donald Trump, "Tweets of December 20, 2018," American Presidency Project, http://presidency.ucsb.edu/documents/tweets-december-20-2018). Although he bombed Iranian nuclear facilities in June 2025, he then wrongly asserted that the entire Iranian nuclear infrastructure had been "obliterated" and pursued an immediate ceasefire between Israel and Iran to avoid further U.S. involvement (Tucker Reals, Haley Ott, Joe Walsh, and Fin Daniel Gómez, "Trump Says Iran-Israel Ceasefire in Effect After Accusing Both Sides of Violating It," CBS News, June 24, 2025, http://cbsnews.com/news/israel-says-iran-violating-ceasefire-trump-announced-will-respond-with-force; and Alexandra Hutzler, "'Obliterated': The Firestorm Over How Trump Described Damage to Iran Nuclear Sites," ABC News, June 25, 2025, http://abcnews.go.com/Politics/obliterated-firestorm-trump-damage-iran-nuclear-sites/story?id=123201314). Trump has applied the same logic to Europe, rejecting a U.S. military presence in Ukraine after a ceasefire: in February 2025 he said, "I'm not going to make security guarantees beyond very much. . . . We're going to have Europe do that. . . . Europe is their next-door neighbor" and in August 2025, that there will be "no going into NATO by Ukraine" (Stephen Collinson, "Trump, Starmer at Odds Over Security Guarantees for Ukraine Ahead of Critical Talks," CNN, February 27, 2025, http://cnn.com/2025/02/27/politics/trump-starmer-security-guarantees-analysis; and Kathryn Armstrong, "'No Going Into Nato by Ukraine,' Says Trump as Zelensky Prepares for White House Talks," BBC News, August 17, 2025, http://bbc.com/news/articles/cm21j1ve817o). In 2024, Trump described a conversation with European leaders: "[Europe] said, 'Well, if we don't pay, are you still going to protect us?' I said, 'Absolutely not.' They couldn't believe the answer. . . . No, I would not protect you. In fact, I would encourage them to do whatever the hell they want." He has also repeatedly questioned U.S. commitments to NATO, especially toward allies on the alliance's eastern flank. "If you're not going to pay, we're not going to defend," he said in 2025. Although Trump was heralded at the June 2025 NATO Summit in The Hague, he cast doubt on his commitment to enforcing Article 5 of the North Atlantic Treaty just before he left the United States. And finally, a week before he attended the June 2025

NATO Summit, when asked if he was committed to Article 5, he said, "Depends on your definition. There's numerous definitions of Article 5" (Kate Sullivan, "Trump Says He Would Encourage Russia to 'Do Whatever the Hell They Want' to Any NATO Country That Doesn't Pay Enough," CNN, February 11, 2024, http://cnn.com/2024/02/10/politics/trump-russia-nato/index.html; Gabe Whisnant and Andrew Stanton, "Donald Trump Draws Red Line for Defending NATO Allies," *Newsweek*, March 6, 2025, http://newsweek.com/trump-weighs-overhaul-nato-commitments-based-defense-spending-report-2040708; and Brett Samuels, "Trump on NATO Mutual Defense Clause: 'If I Didn't Stand With It, I Wouldn't Be Here,'" *The Hill*, June 25, 2025, http://thehill.com/homenews/administration/5368418-trump-nato-article-5-support). Although in September 2025 the Trump administration issued an order that provides Qatar with a mutual defense guarantee similar to NATO's Article 5, this is only an executive order and not a binding treaty. It was also largely in response to Israel's strike on Qatar as Trump was concerned the attack would disrupt Qatar's role as a mediator with Hamas, rather than any serious long-term commitment (Colin Demarest, "U.S. Security Guarantee for Qatar Sparks Jealousy and Confusion," Axios, October 8, 2025, http://axios.com/2025/10/08/trump-qatar-security-guarantee-nato; and Kate Sullivan, "Trump Gave Qatar a Security Guarantee and Isn't Explaining Why," Bloomberg, October 8, 2025, http://bloomberg.com/news/articles/2025-10-08/trump-gave-qatar-a-security-guarantee-and-isn-t-explaining-why).

78. Trump views the Western Hemisphere as an American sphere of influence. He has threatened military action against Mexico, Canada, Greenland, Panama, and Venezuela. He conducted military strikes on suspected drug boats in the Caribbean and deployed an aircraft carrier to the region to increase pressure on Venezuela. He also authorized covert CIA action in Venezuela, and in reference to military strikes Trump said, "We are certainly looking at [strikes on Venezuelan] land now, because we've got the sea very well under control." Trump renamed the Gulf of Mexico the "Gulf of America" and directed the military to target drug cartels in Mexico (Imran Khalid, "The Quiet U.S. Pivot to Latin America," *The Hill*, November 28, 2025, http://thehill.com/opinion/international/5625477-us-latin-america-trade-shift; Matt Murphy and Joshua Cheetham, "U.S. Strikes On Latin American 'Drug Boats': What Do We Know, and Are They Legal?," BBC News, October 20, 2025, http://bbc.com/news/articles/cdjzw3gplv7o; Brad Lendon, "U.S. Navy's 'Most Lethal Combat Platform,' the Carrier USS Gerald R. Ford, Is Being Sent to the Caribbean," CNN, October 25, 2025, http://cnn.com/2025/10/25/americas/aircraft-carrier-uss-gerald-ford-profile-intl-hnk-ml; Julian E. Barnes and Tyler Pager, "Trump Administration Authorizes Covert C.I.A. Action in Venezuela," *New York Times*, October 15, 2025, http://nytimes.com/2025/10/15/us/politics/trump-covert-cia-action-venezuela.html; Ashley Carnahan, "Strikes Against Mexican Drug Cartels Are 'Absolutely' Still on the Table, Says Former President Trump," Fox News, July 23, 2024, http://foxnews.com/media/strikes-against-mexican-drug-cartels-absolutely-still-table-says-former-president-trump; Edward Luce, "Trump, Greenland and the Rebirth of the Monroe Doctrine," *Financial Times*, January 10, 2025, http://ft.com/content/9bbba76a-6b12-4e31-b93e-89cfc3b2e06a; Helene Cooper et al., "Trump Directs Military to Target Foreign Drug Cartels," *New York Times*, August 8, 2025, http://nytimes.com/2025/08/08/us/trump-military-drug-cartels.html; Karen DeYoung, "Trump Revives Monroe Doctrine in U.S. Relations With Western Hemisphere," *Washington Post*, February 28, 2025, http://washingtonpost.com/national-security/2025/02/28/trump-latin-america-monroe-doctrine; Edward Wong, "Trump's Vision: One World, Three Powers?" *New York Times*, May 26, 2025, http://nytimes.com/2025/05/26/us/politics/trump-russia-china.html;

and Charlie Savage, Helene Cooper, and Eric Schmitt, "Is the Trump Administration Building Up to a Military Confrontation With Venezuela?," *New York Times*, August 22, 2025, http://nytimes.com/2025/08/22/us/politics/trump-venezuela-drug-war. html). At the start of Trump's second term, he withdrew from several UN bodies (including UNESCO) and declared that the United States will review "all international organizations" and "all conventions and treaties" to determine if they are also "contrary to the interests of the United States" ("Withdrawing the United States From and Ending Funding to Certain United Nations Organizations and Reviewing United States Support to All International Organizations," Presidential Actions, White House, February 4, 2025, http://whitehouse.gov/presidential-actions/2025/02/withdrawing-the-united-states-from-and-ending-funding-to-certain-united-nations-organizations-and-reviewing-united-states-support-to-all-international-organizations; and Aurelien Breeden and Parin Behrooz, "What to Know About the U.S. Move to Withdraw From UNESCO," *New York Times*, July 23, 2025, Last Updated July 24, 2025, http://nytimes.com/2025/07/23/world/unesco-trump-us-withdrawal.html).

79. Trump's diplomatic style played a significant role in the Israel-Hamas October 2025 ceasefire. According to Martha Raddatz of ABC News, Trump "dispatched diplomats again and again, made threats just in the last few days to Hamas saying again if they did not sign the deal 'All Hell would break loose' and they had the bombing of Iran as an example of that." Trump has also aggressively pressured Israeli Prime Minister Benjamin Netanyahu to agree to the ceasefire (Alexandra Hutzler, "How Much of a Role Did Trump Play in Latest Israel-Hamas Deal?: ANALYSIS," ABC News, October 9, 2025, http://abcnews.go.com/Politics/role-trump-play-latest-israel-hamas-deal-analysis/story?id=126360429; Kevin Shalvey, "Trump Draws International Praise as Broker of Israel-Hamas Deal," ABC News, October 9, 2025, http://abcnews.go.com/International/trump-draws-international-praise-broker-israel-hamas-deal/story?id=126356500; and Shira Rubin, Lior Soroka and Gerry Shih, "Israelis Bristle as Trump Makes Clear Who Calls the Shots in Gaza Truce," *Washington Post*, October 28, 2025, http://washingtonpost.com/world/2025/10/28/gaza-ceasefire-trump-netanyahu-hamas). Another striking example of Trump's pursuit of immediate diplomatic wins came with the sudden ceasefire in Yemen in May 2025. After only seven weeks of U.S. air strikes against Iran-backed Houthi forces (far shorter than the eight-month campaign military planners expected), Trump abruptly declared a halt on May 6, 2025, just in time to tout a "victory" before his Middle East trip, striking a bilateral agreement at the expense of allies, Israel and Britain. Following clashes between India and Pakistan, Trump triumphantly announced a ceasefire and took credit, which the Modi government later denied. Whatever its merits, Trump lifted sanctions on Syria without any interagency analysis of the issue. Trump has also used rapid diplomatic engagement and trade threats to bring about ceasefires in the conflicts between Rwanda and Democratic Republic of Congo and Thailand and Cambodia, and pushed toward a peace deal between Armenia and Azerbaijan (Phil Stewart, Idrees Ali, Humeyra Pamuk, and Erin Banco, "Exclusive: Houthi Ceasefire Followed U.S. Intel Showing Militants Sought Off-Ramp," Reuters, May 13, 2025, http://reuters.com/world/houthi-ceasefire-followed-us-intel-showing-militants-sought-off-ramp-2025-05-13; Hannah Ellis-Petersen, "Uneasy India-Pakistan Ceasefire Holds but Is a Return to War Inevitable?," *The Guardian*, May 20, 2025, http://theguardian.com/world/2025/may/20/uneasy-india-pakistan-ceasefire-holds-but-is-a-return-to-war-inevitable; Rebecca Grant, "Trump Reshapes U.S. Foreign Policy With Wildly Successful, Business-First Middle East Trip," Fox News, May 19, 2025, http://foxnews.com/opinion/trump-reshapes-us-foreign-policy-wildly-successful-business-first-middle-east-trip;

Jeremy Shapiro, "The Bully's Pulpit: Finding Patterns in Trump's Use of Military Force," Article, European Council on Foreign Relations, May 8, 2025, http://ecfr.eu/article/the-bullys-pulpit-finding-patterns-in-trumps-use-of-military-force; "Congo and Rwanda-Backed Rebels Sign Declaration of Principles for a Permanent Ceasefire in the East," CNN, July 19, 2025, http://edition.cnn.com/2025/07/19/africa/congo-rwanda-m23-rebels-ceasefire-intl; John Reed and Sun Narin, "Thailand and Cambodia Set for Ceasefire Talks After Donald Trump Trade Threat," *Financial Times*, July 26, 2025, http://ft.com/content/49daa1b2-3d0e-4fdf-a0fd-c747883ee4be; and Steve Daines, "A Peace Deal for Armenia and Azerbaijan," *Wall Street Journal*, July 29, 2025, http://wsj.com/opinion/a-peace-deal-for-armenia-and-azerbaijan-99373485).

80.   Trump has consistently denigrated the European Union. In February 2025, Trump also said "[the] European Union was formed in order to screw the United States . . . that's the purpose of it, and they've done a good job of it. But now I'm president." His vice president, JD Vance, made similarly critical comments about Europe in the March 2025 leaked Signal messages: "I fully share your loathing of European free-loading. It's PATHETIC." The same month, Trump called the EU "hostile and abusive," and then in May he said the "European Union is, in many ways, nastier than China." And despite claiming that ideology and democracy promotion has no role in its foreign policy, the Trump administration criticizes Europe for its supposed antidemocratic behavior. In a September 2025 speech to the UN General Assembly, Trump told European leaders that "your countries are going to hell" due to their liberal immigration policies (Holly Ellyatt, "Trump Threatens to Slap 25% Tariffs on EU, Says Bloc Was Always Meant to Hurt the U.S.," CNBC, February 27, 2025, Last Updated March 4, 2025, http://cnbc.com/2025/02/27/trump-threatens-25percent-tariffs-on-eu-says-bloc-formed-to-screw-us.html; Jeffrey Goldberg, "The Trump Administration Accidentally Texted Me Its War Plans," *The Atlantic*, March 24, 2025, http://theatlantic.com/politics/archive/2025/03/trump-administration-accidentally-texted-me-its-war-plans/682151; Jeanna Smialek, "Europe Expected a Transactional Trump. It Got Something Else," *New York Times*, March 13, 2025, http://nytimes.com/2025/03/13/world/europe/trump-europe-tariffs-retaliation.html; April Rubin, "Trump Says European Union Is 'Nastier Than China,'" Axios, May 12, 2025, http://axios.com/2025/05/12/trump-european-union-trade-war-china-tariffs; Samuel Samson, "The Need for Civilizational Allies in Europe," Substack, U.S. State Department, May 27, 2025, http://statedept.substack.com/p/the-need-for-civilizational-allies-in-europe; Kathryn Watson and Joe Walsh, "Trump Criticizes European Allies in U.N. Speech: 'Your Countries Are Going to Hell,'" CBS News, Last Updated September 23, 2025, http://cbsnews.com/live-updates/trump-united-nations-general-assembly-speech-unga). Meanwhile, Trump has repeatedly praised authoritarian leaders—especially Russian President Vladimir Putin and Chinese leader Xi Jinping. He has described Putin as a "smart" and "strong" leader since at least 2007, when he said Putin was "doing a great job in rebuilding the image of Russia and also rebuilding Russia." During his 2025 efforts to broker a ceasefire between Russia and Ukraine, Trump claimed Putin was a trustworthy negotiator: "I think he'll keep his word. I've known him for a long time now, and I think he will" ("Larry King Interview With Donald Trump," Transcript, CNN, October 15, 2007, http://transcripts.cnn.com/show/lkl/date/2007-10-15/segment/01; Pippa Crerar, "Trump Says Putin Would Keep His Word on a Ukraine Peace Deal," *The Guardian*, February 27, 2025, http://theguardian.com/politics/2025/feb/27/trump-says-putin-would-keep-his-word-on-a-ukraine-peace-deal; Timothy Naftali, "Trump, Ukraine, and the Limits of Presidential Peacemaking," *Foreign Affairs*, May 2, 2025, http://foreignaffairs.com/united-states/trump-ukraine-and-

limits-presidential-peacemaking; Chris Cillizza, "Donald Trump Just Can't Stop Praising Vladimir Putin," CNN, March 28, 2022, http://cnn.com/2022/03/28/politics/trump-putin-ukraine-russia-smart). Trump evidently respects Xi too. In 2024, he described Xi as a "brilliant guy" who "controls 1.4 billion people with an iron fist." Trump also stated, "I had a very strong relationship with him [Xi]. He was actually a really good, I don't want to say friend—I don't want to act foolish, 'he was my friend'—but I got along with him great. He stayed at Mar-a-Lago with me, so we got to know each other great" ("Joe Rogan Interview With Donald Trump," *Joe Rogan Experience* podcast, YouTube, October 25, 2024, http://youtube.com/watch?v=hBMoPUAeLnY&ab_channel=PowerfulJRE; and James Taranto, "Weekend Interview: Trump Tangles With the Journal's Editors," *Wall Street Journal*, October 18, 2024, http://wsj.com/opinion/donald-trump-the-bully-with-a-heart-of-gold-2024-presidential-election-dd922dd6).

81. In his second term, Trump has flatlined U.S. defense spending growth while refocusing on the American Homeland and Western Hemisphere. His second term's first budget kept the Pentagon's base funding essentially unchanged—a move that left military spending reduced in real terms. Simultaneously, Trump directed a massive boost to domestic security: his FY2026 plan increased Department of Homeland Security funding by 65 percent, and funneled resources to border defense against what he called an "invasion" of criminals. Consistent with this focus, Trump often stresses avoiding costly military interventions that could kill U.S. troops—boasting that under his leadership America measures success not just by victories won but by "the wars that we end" and, most important, "the wars we never get into" (Editorial Board, "Trump Isn't Rebuilding the U.S. Military," *Wall Street Journal*, July 11, 2025, http://wsj.com/opinion/trump-isnt-rebuilding-the-u-s-military-national-security-defense-spending-266b41e6; "Committee Releases FY26 Defense Bill," Press Release, United States House Committee on Appropriations, June 9, 2025, http://appropriations.house.gov/news/press-releases/committee-releases-fy26-defense-bill; Joe Gould, Connor O'Brien, Eric Bazail-Eimil, and Robbie Gramer, "Making Sense of Trump's Defense Spending Math," *Politico*, May 5, 2025, http://politico.com/newsletters/national-security-daily/2025/05/05/making-sense-of-trumps-defense-spending-math-00329045; "The White House Office of Management and Budget Releases the President's Fiscal Year 2026 Skinny Budget," Briefings & Statements, Trump White House, May 2, 2025, http://whitehouse.gov/briefings-statements/2025/05/the-white-house-office-of-management-and-budget-releases-the-presidents-fiscal-year-2026-skinny-budget; and "The Inaugural Address," Remarks, Trump White House, January 20, 2025, http://whitehouse.gov/remarks/2025/01/the-inaugural-address).

82. It may be that Trump's June 22, 2025, attack on Iran's nuclear facilities is a singularity, his only use of substantial military force during his entire second term. Israel had eliminated Iran's air defenses, there was little risk of any U.S. casualties, and he had a brief opportunity to "obliterate" Iran's nuclear weapons potential, a strategic achievement that none of his predecessors had accomplished. That nexus is unlikely to present itself again during his remaining years in office (Jonathan Swan and Maggie Haberman, "With Decision to Bomb Iran, Trump Injects U.S. Into Middle East Conflict," *New York Times*, June 21, 2025, http://nytimes.com/2025/06/21/world/middleeast/us-bomb-iran-trump-war.html; and Aamer Madhani and Josh Boak, "A Whirlwind 48 Hours: How Trump's Israel-Iran Ceasefire Agreement Came Together," Associated Press, June 25, 2025, http://apnews.com/article/trump-iran-israel-ceasefire-agreement-terms-b5fc5cc8a8c32b4899646130b496798a).

83. Trump unequivocally opposes U.S. efforts to tackle climate change, instead prioritizing energy independence and ramping up fossil fuel production. In an address to the UN General Assembly in September 2025, Trump called climate change the "greatest con job ever perpetrated on the world" and asserted that "the carbon footprint is a hoax made up by people with evil intentions." During Trump's January 2025 inaugural address, he declared, "We will be a rich nation again, and it is that liquid gold under our feet that will help to do it." Trump has consistently opposed efforts to limit the damage from climate change, such as withdrawing from the Paris Climate Agreement (twice), rescinding Biden-era executive orders on climate change, removing renewable incentives like the electric vehicle tax credit, and tearing up greenhouse gas emission standards imposed by the Environmental Protection Agency. Trump has also encouraged fossil fuel production such as by opening more federal land to oil and gas drilling. In April 2025, he signed an executive order to end all "burdensome and ideologically motivated 'climate change' or energy policies that threaten American energy dominance and our economic and national security" (Eli Stokols, "Trump Sets Foreign Policy Agenda For His Successor," *Politico*, October 3, 2025, http://politico.com/news/2025/10/03/trump-sets-foreign-policy-agenda-for-his-successor-00591744; Josephine Walker, "'Greatest con job': Trump Pushes Climate Change Denial in United Nations Speech," Axios, September 23, 2025, http://axios.com/2025/09/23/trump-united-nations-climate-change-scam; "The Inaugural Address," Remarks, Trump White House, January 20, 2025, http://whitehouse.gov/remarks/2025/01/the-inaugural-address; Melina Walling, "Here's What to Know About Trump's Executive Actions on Climate and Environment," *PBS News Hour*, January 27, 2025, http://pbs.org/newshour/nation/heres-what-to-know-about-trumps-executive-actions-on-climate-and-environment; Alex Guillén, "Trump Administration Moves to Repeal Climate 'Holy Grail,'" *Politico*, July 29, 2025, http://politico.com/news/2025/07/29/epa-to-revoke-2009-finding-that-climate-pollution-endangers-humans-00476166; David Gelles, Lisa Friedman, and Brad Plumer, "'Full-on Fight Club': How Trump Is Crushing U.S. Climate Policy," *New York Times*, March 2, 2025, Last Updated August 1, 2025, http://nytimes.com/2025/03/02/climate/trump-us-climate-policy-changes.html). He also completely dismisses human rights concerns, such as dismantling USAID support for human rights programs globally, or in his Riyadh speech, where he said, "far too many American presidents have been afflicted with the notion that it's our job to look into the souls of foreign leaders and use U.S. policy to dispense justice for their sins. . . . I believe it is God's job to sit in judgement—my job [is] to defend America and to promote the fundamental interests of stability, prosperity, and peace" ("In Riyadh, President Trump Charts the Course for a Prosperous Future in the Middle East," May 13, 2025, Articles, Trump White House, http://whitehouse.gov/articles/2025/05/in-riyadh-president-trump-charts-the-course-for-a-prosperous-future-in-the-middle-east; David Smith, "Trump's Foreign Policy Is Not So Unusual for the U.S.—He Just Drops the Facade of Moral Leadership," *The Guardian*, May 26, 2025, http://theguardian.com/us-news/2025/may/26/trump-foreign-policy-moral-leadership; and Suzanne Nossel, "The Great Dismantling," *Foreign Policy*, July 24, 2025, http://foreignpolicy.com/2025/07/24/liberal-international-order-dismantling-trump-usaid-state-department-human-rights).

84. In September 2018, Trump declared, "We reject globalism and embrace the doctrine of patriotism. . . . The U.S. will always choose independence and cooperation over global governance, control and domination." Trump's pursuit of raw national interest is also visible in his insistence on bilateral dealmaking, rather than multilateral deals, on the grounds that they give the United States more direct leverage. In January 2017, Trump withdrew from the Trans-Pacific Partnership, arguing he is "paving the way for new one-on-one

trade deals that protect and defend the American worker. And believe me, we're going to have a lot of trade deals. But they'll be one-on-one. There won't be a whole big mash pot" (W.J. Hennigan, "'We Reject Globalism.' President Trump Took 'America First' to the United Nations," *Time*, September 25, 2018, http://time.com/5406130/we-reject-globalism-president-trump-took-america-first-to-the-united-nations; "Building the Wall," Transcript, *Wall Street Journal*, January 30, 2017, http://wsj.com/articles/building-the-wall-1485796043; Kiron Skinner, "Trump's New American Doctrine Means Peace Through Strength Has Returned," Fox News, June 30, 2025, http://foxnews.com/opinion/trumps-new-american-doctrine-means-peace-through-strength-has-returned; and Walter Russell Mead, "Trump Seeks to Remake the World," *Wall Street Journal*, June 30, 2025, http://wsj.com/opinion/trump-seeks-to-remake-the-world-foreign-policy-4e41c836).

85. In February 2017, when Trump was asked why he respects Putin given that he is a "killer," Trump responded, "You think our country's so innocent?" Trump has also refused to rule out using military force to conquer Greenland (Sophie Tatum, "Trump Defends Putin: 'You Think Our Country's So Innocent?'," CNN, February 6, 2017, http://cnn.com/2017/02/04/politics/donald-trump-vladimir-putin; Will Weissert and Zeke Miller, "Trump Refuses to Rule Out Use of Military Force to Take Control of Greenland and the Panama Canal," Associated Press, January 7, 2025, http://apnews.com/article/trump-biden-offshore-drilling-gulf-of-america-fa66f8d072eb39c00a8128a8941ede75; and Jemima Kelly, "The Power and the Glory of Profanity," *Financial Times*, June 29, 2025, http://ft.com/content/97b59508-9c37-48ea-b673-d048289faac8).

86. Ravi Agrawal, "Trump Is Ushering in a More Transactional World," *Foreign Policy*, January 7, 2025, http://foreignpolicy.com/2025/01/07/trump-transactional-global-system-us-allies-markets-tariffs; and Emma Ashford, "If Trump Is Neither Hawk Nor Dove, What Is He?," *Foreign Policy*, July 14, 2025, http://foreignpolicy.com/2025/07/14/trump-andrew-jackson-jacksonianism-hawk-dove.

87. "President Trump Is Leading With Peace Through Strength," Articles, Trump White House, March 4, 2025, http://whitehouse.gov/articles/2025/03/president-trump-is-leading-with-peace-through-strength; Ashley Parker and Michael Scherer, "'I Run the Country and the World,'" *The Atlantic*, April 28, 2025, http://theatlantic.com/magazine/archive/2025/06/trump-second-term-comeback/682573; and Emma Colton, "Trump White House Celebrates Latest Chapter of Wins at 200-Day Mark," Fox News, August 7, 2025, http://foxnews.com/politics/trump-white-house-celebrates-latest-chapter-wins-200-day-mark.

88. "Fact Sheet: President Donald J. Trump Declares National Emergency to Increase Our Competitive Edge, Protect Our Sovereignty, and Strengthen Our National and Economic Security," Fact Sheet, Trump White House, April 2, 2025, http://whitehouse.gov/fact-sheets/2025/04/fact-sheet-president-donald-j-trump-declares-national-emergency-to-increase-our-competitive-edge-protect-our-sovereignty-and-strengthen-our-national-and-economic-security; Peter Foster, Amy Borrett, Andy Bounds, and Ilya Gridneff, "Donald Trump Reaps $50bn Tariff Haul as World 'Chickens Out,'" *Financial Times*, July 16, 2025, http://ft.com/content/82e32f7c-47e2-4e96-bb53-a58377e18aa9; "TRUMP EFFECT: A Running List of New U.S. Investment in President Trump's Second Term," Articles, Trump White House, August 15, 2025, http://whitehouse.gov/articles/2025/08/trump-effect-a-running-list-of-new-u-s-investment-in-president-trumps-second-term; "Fact Sheet: President Donald J. Trump Secures Unprecedented U.S.–Japan Strategic Trade And Investment Agreement," Fact Sheets, Trump White House, July 23, 2025,

http://whitehouse.gov/fact-sheets/2025/07/fact-sheet-president-donald-j-trump-secures-unprecedented-u-s-japan-strategic-trade-and-investment-agreement; "PROMISES MADE, PROMISES KEPT: Border Security Achieved in Fewer Than 100 Days," Articles, Trump White House, April 28, 2025, http://whitehouse.gov/articles/2025/04/promises-made-promises-kept-border-security-achieved-in-fewer-than-100-days; Camilo Montoya-Galvez, "Amid Trump Crackdown, Illegal Border Crossings Plunge to Levels Not Seen in Decades," CBS News, March 3, 2025, http://cbsnews.com/news/illegal-crossings-plunge-to-levels-not-seen-in-decades-amid-trump-crackdown; Josh Marcus, "Trump Ups Number of Wars he Claims to Have Ended From 7 to 10: 'If You Think About Pre-Wars,'" *The Independent*, August 22, 2025, http://independent.co.uk/news/world/americas/us-politics/trump-ended-wars-ukraine-russia-noble-peace-prize-b2813227.html; Steven Erlanger and Lara Jakes, "In a Win for Trump, NATO Agrees to a Big Increase in Military Spending," *New York Times*, June 25, 2025, http://nytimes.com/2025/06/25/world/europe/nato-increase-military-spending-trump.html; and "Iran's Nuclear Facilities Have Been Obliterated—and Suggestions Otherwise Are Fake News," Articles, Trump White House, June 25, 2025, http://whitehouse.gov/articles/2025/06/irans-nuclear-facilities-have-been-obliterated-and-suggestions-otherwise-are-fake-news.

89. Karen Tumulty, "Trump Swerves and Swaggers on the World Stage," *Washington Post*, September 28, 2025, http://washingtonpost.com/politics/2025/09/28/trump-un-foreign-policy-doctrine-.

90. See Trump's May 13, 2025 Riyadh speech: "In Riyadh, President Trump Charts the Course for a Prosperous Future in the Middle East," May 13, 2025, Articles, Trump White House, http://whitehouse.gov/articles/2025/05/in-riyadh-president-trump-charts-the-course-for-a-prosperous-future-in-the-middle-east; Greg Myre, "Trump's Foreign Policy: Deals With Allies Over Diplomacy with Rivals," NPR, May 28, 2025, http://npr.org/2025/05/28/nx-s1-5406774/trumps-foreign-policy-deals-with-allies-over-diplomacy-with-rivals; and Betsy Klein, Jeff Zeleny, Kaitlan Collins, and Donald Judd, "7 Takeaways From Trump's Middle East Trip," CNN, May 16, 2025, http://cnn.com/2025/05/16/politics/trump-middle-east-takeaways.

91. Trump has threatened to use tariffs against the BRICS nations for their anti-American policies, against Thailand and Cambodia to resolve their dispute, against Russia to pressure Moscow into a Ukraine ceasefire, and against India for purchasing Russian energy. These would be geoeconomic actions as defined as "the use of economic instruments to promote and defend national interests, and to produce beneficial geopolitical results; and the effects of other nations' economic actions on a country's geopolitical goals," quoted from Robert D. Blackwill and Jennifer M. Harris, *War By Other Means: Geoeconomics and Statecraft* (Cambridge, MA: Belknap Press, 2016), 20. See also Eric Bazail-Eimil and Nahal Toosi, "Tariffs Top Trump's Natsec Toolbox," *Politico*, July 10, 2025, http://politico.com/newsletters/national-security-daily/2025/07/10/tariffs-top-trumps-natsec-toolbox-00447505; Ben Johansen, "Trump Leans Into Trade Threats to Try to Stop Cambodia-Thailand Clashes," Politico Pro, July 26, 2025, http://subscriber.politicopro.com/article/2025/07/26/trump-cambodia-thailand-clash-00478150; Kevin Liptak and Elisabeth Buchwald, "Trump Threatens India With 50% Tariff as Negotiations Fizzle and Modi Keeps Importing Russian Oil," CNN, August 6, 2025, http://cnn.com/2025/08/06/politics/india-tariffs-trump-russian-oil; Laura Gozzi, "Trump Threatens Russia With Tariffs While Unveiling Ukraine Weapons Plan," BBC News, July 14, 2025, http://bbc.co.uk/news/articles/czdv20v9lp1o; "Fact Sheet:

President Donald J. Trump Declares National Emergency"; and Emma Colton and Brooke Singman, "Trump Vows to Lead 'Golden Age of America' in Victory Speech: 'Fix Everything,'" Fox News, November 6, 2024, http://foxnews.com/politics/trump-vows-lead-golden-age-america-victory-speech-fix-everything.

92. Ross Douthat, "Trump Only Sees the World Through Deals," *New York Times*, May 17, 2025, http://nytimes.com/2025/05/17/opinion/trump-foreign-policy-doctrine-deal.html; and Eric Schmitt, "U.S. Is Withdrawing Hundreds of Troops From Syria," *New York Times*, April 17, 2025, http://nytimes.com/2025/04/17/us/politics/us-withdrawing-troops-syria.html.

93. Stacie E. Goddard, "The Rise and Fall of Great-Power Competition," *Foreign Affairs*, April 22, 2025, http://foreignaffairs.com/united-states/rise-and-fall-great-power-competition; Edward Luce, "Trump, Greenland and the Rebirth of the Monroe Doctrine," *Financial Times*, January 10, 2025, http://ft.com/content/9bbba76a-6b12-4e31-b93e-89cfc3b2e06a; Karen DeYoung, "Trump Revives Monroe Doctrine in U.S. Relations With Western Hemisphere," *Washington Post*, February 28, 2025, http://washingtonpost.com/national-security/2025/02/28/trump-latin-america-monroe-doctrine; and Edward Wong, "Trump's Vision: One World, Three Powers?" *New York Times*, May 26, 2025, http://nytimes.com/2025/05/26/us/politics/trump-russia-china.html.

94. Thomas P.M. Barnett, "The Theory Behind Trump's Gunboat Diplomacy," *Politico*, October 25, 2025, http://politico.com/news/magazine/2025/10/25/trump-venezuela-monroe-doctrine-00618322.

95. See endnote on Trumpism Pillar Six.

96. "Withdrawing the United States From and Ending Funding to Certain United Nations Organizations and Reviewing United States Support to All International Organizations," Presidential Actions, Trump White House, February 4, 2025, http://whitehouse.gov/presidential-actions/2025/02/withdrawing-the-united-states-from-and-ending-funding-to-certain-united-nations-organizations-and-reviewing-united-states-support-to-all-international-organizations; Patrick Wintour, "UN Faces $500M Budget Cut and 20% Job Losses After Big Drop in U.S. Funding," *The Guardian*, September 18, 2025, http://theguardian.com/world/2025/sep/18/united-nations-un-2026-budget-job-losses-us-funding-cuts; and James Landale, "Seven Years Ago Trump's UN Audience Laughed, This Year They Were Silent," BBC News, September 23, 2025, http://bbc.com/news/articles/c179p4wvz29o.

97. Lazaro Gamio, Tony Romm, and Agnes Chang, "Tracking Trump's New Tariffs on Every Country," *New York Times*, Last Updated August 11, 2025, http://nytimes.com/interactive/2025/07/28/business/economy/trump-tariff-tracker.html.

98. Ibid; and Rebecca Grant, "Trump Scores Four Big Wins With Xi, but Has One Big Miss," Fox News, October 30, 2025, http://foxnews.com/opinion/trump-scores-four-big-wins-xi-has-one-big-miss.

99. "Fact Sheet: The United States and European Union Reach Massive Trade Deal," Fact Sheets, Trump White House, July 28, 2025, http://whitehouse.gov/fact-sheets/2025/07/fact-sheet-the-united-states-and-european-union-reach-massive-trade-deal.

100. Paul Kirby, "Trump Says Nato's New 5% Defense Spending Pledge a 'Big Win'," BBC News, June 25, 2025, http://bbc.com/news/articles/cj4en8djwyko; and David I. Goldman, "The Transatlantic Tussle—A Historical Case Study on How to Handle NATO," War on

the Rocks, March 18, 2019, http://warontherocks.com/2019/03/the-transatlantic-tussle-a-historical-case-study-on-how-to-handle-nato.

101. Daniel Michaels and Lara Seligman, "U.S. Sells $1 Billion in Arms to Europe for Ukraine, Sealing Shift in Weapons Pipeline," *Wall Street Journal*, August 5, 2025, http://wsj.com/world/europe/u-s-sells-1-billion-in-arms-to-europe-for-ukraine-sealing-shift-in-approach-73dea030; "Fact Sheet: President Donald J. Trump Addresses Threats to the United States by the Government of the Russian Federation," Fact Sheets, Trump White House, August 6, 2025, http://whitehouse.gov/fact-sheets/2025/08/fact-sheet-president-donald-j-trump-addresses-threats-to-the-united-states-by-the-government-of-the-russian-federation; "U.S. Treasury Sanctions Major Russian Oil Companies, Calls on Moscow to Immediately Agree to Ceasefire," Press Release, U.S. Department of the Treasury, October 22, 2025, http://home.treasury.gov/news/press-releases/sb0290; Bernd Debusmann Jr, Max Matza and Ian Aikman, "Trump Says Putin Talks 'Don't Go Anywhere' as He Imposes New Sanctions," BBC News, October 22, 2025, http://bbc.com/news/articles/cd6758pn6ylo; "Iran's Nuclear Facilities Have Been Obliterated—and Suggestions Otherwise Are Fake News," Articles, Trump White House, June 25, 2025, http://whitehouse.gov/articles/2025/06/irans-nuclear-facilities-have-been-obliterated-and-suggestions-otherwise-are-fake-news; Brooke Singman, "Iran, Israel and U.S. Agree That Islamic Republic Nuclear Sites Were 'Badly Damaged' Despite Leaked Intel Report," Fox News, June 26, 2025, http://foxnews.com/politics/iran-israel-us-agree-islamic-republic-nuclear-sites-were-badly-damaged-despite-leaked-intel-report; Alex Nitzberg, "Trump Announces India and Pakistan Agreed to Ceasefire," Fox News, May 10, 2025, http://foxnews.com/world/trump-announces-india-pakistan-agreed-ceasefire; Stepheny Price and Trey Yingst, "Trump Announces Historic Iran and Israel Ceasefire Agreement to End '12 Day War,'" Fox News, June 23, 2025, http://foxnews.com/us/trump-announces-historic-iran-israel-ceasefire-agreement-end-12-day-war; Greg Norman, "Thailand, Cambodia Reach Ceasefire Deal to End Conflict That Displaced 260K, Trump Says," Fox News, July 28, 2025, http://foxnews.com/politics/thailand-cambodia-reach-ceasefire-deal-end-conflict-displaced-260k-trump-says; Alexandra Koch, "Trump and Rubio Secure Rwanda-Congo Peace Treaty Amid Pakistan's Nobel Prize Nomination," Fox News, June 20, 2025, http://foxnews.com/world/trump-rubio-secure-rwanda-congo-peace-treaty-amid-pakistans-nobel-prize-nomination; and Morgan Phillips, "Trump Brings Peace to Caucasus: Inside the Armenia–Azerbaijan Deal 30 Years in the Making," Fox News, August 14, 2025, http://foxnews.com/politics/trump-brings-peace-caucasus-inside-armenia-azerbaijan-deal-30-years-making.

102. Kathryn Watson, "Trump Vows U.S. Help in Settling Sudan War, at Request of Saudi Crown Prince," CBS News, November 19, 2025, http://cbsnews.com/news/trump-sudan-saudi-arabia-mohammed-bin-salman-kennedy-center.

103. "A New Beginning for the Middle East," *The Economist*, October 9, 2025, http://economist.com/leaders/2025/10/09/a-new-beginning-for-the-middle-east; and Editorial Board, "Donald Trump and Peace in the Mideast," *Washington Post*, October 9, 2025, http://washingtonpost.com/opinions/2025/10/09/gaza-israel-hamas-peace-plan-trump.

104. Mariel Ferragamo, "A Guide to the Gaza Peace Deal," Article, Council on Foreign Relations, Last Updated October 24, 2025, http://cfr.org/article/guide-trumps-twenty-point-gaza-peace-deal.

105. Walter Russell Mead, "Trump's Triumphal March," *Wall Street Journal*, October 13, 2025, http://wsj.com/opinion/trumps-triumphal-march-5bb61e77.

106. Farnaz Fassihi, "In Major Breakthrough, UN Security Council Adopts U.S. Peace Plan for Gaza," *New York Times*, November 17, 2025, http://nytimes.com/2025/11/17/world/middleeast/un-security-council-gaza-peace-plan.html.

107. Hal Brands, "Trump Is Opening a New Chapter in U.S. Foreign Policy," Bloomberg, July 8, 2025, http://bloomberg.com/opinion/articles/2025-07-08/trump-doctrine-puts-american-power-front-and-center.

108. Stephen M. Walt, "The Top 10 Trump Administration Foreign-Policy Mistakes," *Foreign Policy*, September 10, 2025, http://foreignpolicy.com/2025/09/10/top-10-trump-administration-foreign-policy-mistakes; Thomas L. Friedman agrees: Thomas L. Friedman, "Trump's Gilded Gut Instinct," *New York Times*, June 3, 2025, http://nytimes.com/2025/06/03/opinion/trump-president-governing-ruler.html; Emma Ashford, "Trump Lacks the Patience for Peace," *Foreign Policy*, June 20, 2025, http://foreignpolicy.com/2025/06/20/trump-iran-israel-ukraine-russia-peace-patience; Frank Bruni, "The (Gaudy) Tie That Binds Trump and Bezos," *New York Times*, June 30, 2025, http://nytimes.com/2025/06/30/opinion/trump-bezos-sanchez-iran.html; Stephen M. Walt, "Why Trump Keeps Betraying His Base," *Foreign Policy*, July 21, 2025, http://foreignpolicy.com/2025/07/21/trump-betray-base-foreign-policy-epstein-putin-ukraine-iran-syria-war; and Stephen M. Walt, "Trump's Missed Opportunities Are Piling Up," *Foreign Policy*, July 29, 2025, http://foreignpolicy.com/2025/07/29/trumps-missed-opportunities-are-piling-up.

109. Eric Lipton et al., "Anatomy of Two Giant Deals: The U.A.E. Got Chips. The Trump Team Got Crypto Riches," *New York Times*, September 15, 2025, http://nytimes.com/2025/09/15/us/politics/trump-uae-chips-witkoff-world-liberty.html; Carlos Lozada, "The One Question Trump Always Wants the Answer To," *New York Times*, June 27, 2025, http://nytimes.com/2025/06/27/opinion/trump-iran-israel-policy.html; and Eric Lipton, "The Trumps Get Richer," *New York Times*, May 14, 2025, http://nytimes.com/2025/05/14/briefing/trump-family-business.html.

110. In the words of Stephen Walt, "[Trump] doesn't prepare, doesn't have subordinates lay the groundwork beforehand, and arrives at each meeting not knowing what he wants or where his red lines are. He has no strategy and isn't interested in the details, so he just wings it" (Stephen M. Walt, "Trump Has No Idea How to Do Diplomacy," *Foreign Policy*, August 19, 2025, http://foreignpolicy.com/2025/08/19/trump-diplomacy-putin-ukraine-europe; and Luke Broadwater and Julian E. Barnes, "'Flying Blind': Trump Strips Government of Expertise at a High-Stakes Moment," *New York Times*, August 21, 2025, http://nytimes.com/2025/08/21/us/politics/trump-government-expertise.html). Trump has repeatedly expressed a desire to win the Nobel Peace Prize. "If I were named Obama, I would have had the Nobel prize given to me in 10 seconds," Trump said in 2024. This year, ahead of the Nobel Committee's announcement, Trump said that "it will be a big insult to our country" if he does not win and declared that "I deserve [the Nobel Peace Prize], but they will never give it to me." The White House blasted the decision of the Nobel Committee to award Venezuelan pro-democracy activist María Corina Machado, saying that the "Nobel Committee proved they place politics over peace" (Trevor Hunnicutt and Steve Holland, "Trump Says He Spoke With Machado After White House Criticizes Nobel Snub," Reuters, October 11, 2025, http://reuters.com/world/americas/white-house-says-nobel-committee-places-politics-over-peace-2025-10-10; "Trump Told Norwegian Minister He Wants Nobel Prize, Newspaper Says," Reuters, August 14, 2025, http://reuters.com/world/asia-pacific/trump-

told-norwegian-minister-he-wants-nobel-prize-newspaper-says-2025-08-14; Michael Birnbaum, "Trump Badly Wants a Nobel Peace Prize. Most On the Committee Oppose Him," *Washington Post*, August 25, 2025, http://washingtonpost.com/politics/2025/08/25/trump-nobel-peace-prize; Kayla Epstein, "White House Blasts Nobel Committee for Not Awarding Peace Prize to Trump," BBC News, October 10, 2025, http://bbc.com/news/articles/c7842qg15p6o; Alex Gangtiano, "Trump: It Would Be 'An Insult To Our Country' If He Doesn't Get Nobel Peace Prize," *The Hill*, September 30, 2025, http://thehill.com/homenews/administration/5529126-donald-trump-nobel-peace-prize-insult; Andrew Roth, "Truly, Madly, Deeply: Trump's Desire for a Nobel Peace Prize Is Driving Diplomacy," *The Guardian*, October 9, 2025, http://theguardian.com/us-news/2025/oct/09/trump-nobel-peace-prize; and Mike Pesoli and Michelle L. Price, "Trump's Quest for The Nobel Peace Prize Falls Short Again Despite High-Profile Nominations," AP News, October 10, 2025, http://apnews.com/article/donald-trump-misses-out-on-nobel-peace-prize-729973788d8953da9af1cbc136232e96). During his second term, Trump has pursued family commercial benefit by accepting a $400 million Qatari luxury jet for Air Force One use that would transfer to his presidential library upon leaving office, while his family's crypto ventures (including World Liberty Financial and the $Trump meme coin) have generated over $800 million as his administration loosened cryptocurrency regulations (David Gauthier-Villars et al., "Inside the Trump Family's Global Crypto Cash Machine," Reuters, October 28, 2025, http://reuters.com/investigations/inside-trump-familys-global-crypto-cash-machine-2025-10-28; Vivian Nereim, "Trump Family's Business Ties to Saudi Arabia Raise Ethics Worries," *New York Times*, November 18, 2025, http://nytimes.com/2025/11/18/world/middleeast/trump-family-business-saudi-arabia.html; Kat Lonsdort, "Trump Administration Officially Accepts Jet From Qatar for Use as Air Force One," NPR, May 21, 2025, http://npr.org/2025/05/21/nx-s1-5406420/trump-accepts-qatar-plane-air-force-one; Jacon Knutson, "Foreign Officials Spent 'Hundreds of Thousands' at Trump's DC Hotel," Axios, November 14, 2022, http://axios.com/2022/11/14/trump-dc-hotel-foreign-officials; Bernd Debusmann Jr., "Jared Kushner Defends Controversial $2bn Saudi Investment," BBC News, February 14, 2024, http://bbc.com/news/world-us-canada-68296877; Zach Everson, "MGX Cites 'Compliance History' in Picking Brand New Trump-Linked Stablecoin USD1 for $2 Billion Binance Deal," *Forbes*, October 2, 2025, http://forbes.com/sites/zacheverson/2025/10/02/mgx-usd1-binance-trump-stablecoin-world-liberty-financial; Luke Broadwater, "Trump Received Millions From Foreign Governments as President, Report Finds," *New York Times*, January 4, 2024, http://nytimes.com/2024/01/04/us/politics/trump-hotels-foreign-business-report.html; Julia Harte, "Exclusive: Foreign Government Leases at Trump World Tower Stir More Emoluments Concerns," Reuters, May 3, 2025, http://reuters.com/article/world/us-politics/exclusive-foreign-government-leases-at-trump-world-tower-stir-more-emoluments-c-idUSKCN1S80PO; and Zachary Cohen and Kara Scannell, "China Spent Over $5.5 Million at Trump Properties While He Was in Office, Documents Show," CNN, January 4, 2024, http://edition.cnn.com/2024/01/04/politics/trump-properties-china-foreign-payments).

111. Henry A. Kissinger quoted in Chas W. Freeman, Jr., *The Diplomat's Dictionary* (Washington, DC: U.S. Institute of Peace Press, 1997), 194.

112. Amanda Taub, "The Trump Doctrine: The World Is a Zero-Sum Game," *New York Times*, March 7, 2025, http://nytimes.com/2025/03/07/world/trump-doctrine-zero-sum-game.html.

113. Jan-Werner Müller, "Trump's Megalomaniac White House Project Fits a Global Trend Among Far-Right Populists," *The Guardian*, October 26, 2025, http://theguardian.com/commentisfree/2025/oct/26/trump-white-house-far-right-populism; Ed Kilgore, "Trump's Megalomania Undermines Biden Blame Game," *New York Magazine*, April 30, 2025, http://nymag.com/intelligencer/article/trumps-megalomania-undermines-biden-blame-game.html.

114. Joseph Krauss, "For Trump the Peace Negotiator, Might Makes Right. History Offers Different Lessons," Associated Press, March 10, 2025, http://apnews.com/article/trump-diplomacy-war-israel-hamas-russia-ukraine-history-1e35f451708a51cb6454ce315bef5c7e; and Sarang Shidore "Spheres of Influence Are Not the Answer," *Foreign Policy*, May 28, 2025, http://foreignpolicy.com/2025/05/28/spheres-of-influence-great-powers.

115. Gerard Baker, "Trump Is Trashing America's Reputation," *Wall Street Journal*, April 7, 2025, http://wsj.com/opinion/trump-is-trashing-americas-global-good-name-foreign-policy-tariffs-trade-economy-b2d63350; and Howard W. French, "The U.S. Can No Longer Stave Off Competition From China," *Foreign Policy*, July 18, 2025, http://foreignpolicy.com/2025/07/18/trump-trade-letters-tariffs-us-china-competition.

116. "Donald Trump Has Purged One of the CIA's Most Senior Russia Analysts," *The Economist*, August 21, 2025, http://economist.com/united-states/2025/08/21/donald-trump-has-purged-one-of-the-cias-most-senior-russia-analysts; Stephen M. Walt, "Trump Has No Idea How to Do Diplomacy," *Foreign Policy*, August 19, 2025, http://foreignpolicy.com/2025/08/19/trump-diplomacy-putin-ukraine-europe; and Luke Broadwater and Julian E. Barnes, "'Flying Blind': Trump Strips Government of Expertise at a High-Stakes Moment," *New York Times*, August 21, 2025, http://nytimes.com/2025/08/21/us/politics/trump-government-expertise.html.

117. Steven Benen, "Hegseth's Pentagon Purge Goes From Bad to Worse as the Air Force's Chief of Staff Exits," MSNBC, August 19, 2025, http://msnbc.com/rachel-maddow-show/maddowblog/pete-hegseth-pentagon-purge-air-force-david-allvin-rcna225831; and Idrees Ali and Jonathan Landay, "In Latest Purge, Hegseth Removes Head of Pentagon Intelligence Agency, Other Senior Officials," Reuters, August 22, 2025, http://reuters.com/world/us/latest-purge-hegseth-removes-head-pentagon-intelligence-agency-other-senior-2025-08-22.

118. Josh Marcus, "Trump Ups Number of Wars He Claims to Have Ended From 7 to 10: 'If you Think About Pre-Wars,'" *The Independent*, August 22, 2025, http://independent.co.uk/news/world/americas/us-politics/trump-ended-wars-ukraine-russia-noble-peace-prize-b2813227.html; and Jenny Gross et al., "Trump Says He's Ended 6 (or 7) Wars. Here's Some Context," *New York Times*, August 19, 2025, http://nytimes.com/2025/08/19/world/europe/trump-six-wars-fact-check.html.

119. Zachary B. Wolf, "Did the U.S. Commit a War Crime in the Caribbean? Here's What We Know," CNN, December 2, 2025, http://cnn.com/2025/12/02/politics/boat-strike-controversy-legal-experts; Michael Gold, "Lawmakers Suggest Follow-Up Boat Strike Could Be a War Crime," *New York Times*, November 30, 2025, http://nytimes.com/2025/11/30/us/politics/trump-boat-strikes-war-crime.html; Tara Suter, "Ex-Defense Chief Panetta Says He Doesn't 'Think There's Any Question' Second Strike Was War Crime," *The Hill*, December 1, 2025, http://thehill.com/policy/defense/5628310-leon-panetta-us-strike-alleged-drug-boat.

120. Daniel Dale, "Fact Check: Trump and the Case of the Nonexistent $600 Billion EU 'Gift,'" CNN, August 22, 2025, http://cnn.com/2025/08/22/politics/fact-check-trump-eu-us-gift; Ben Werschkul, "Trump's New Trade World Is Built Around Recent Deals. The Problem: We Still Don't Know Many Details," Yahoo Finance, August 9, 2025, http://finance.yahoo.com/news/trumps-new-trade-world-is-built-around-recent-deals-the-problem-we-still-dont-know-many-details-114505174.html; Alexander Ward and Meridith McGraw, "Trump Pivots Second Term Toward Foreign Policy," *Wall Street Journal*, October 30, 2025, http://wsj.com/politics/policy/trump-pivots-second-term-toward-foreign-policy-08d66474; and Michael B.G. Froman, "Celebrating the Arsonist," *The World This Week*, Council on Foreign Relations, October 31, 2025, http://cfr.org/article/celebrating-arsonist.

121. Erin Doherty, "Trump Views Foreign Investment Pledges as Gifts. Trade Partners Say That's Way Off the Mark," CNBC, August 6, 2025, http://cnbc.com/2025/08/06/trump-trade-tariffs-investment-pledge.html.

122. Vivek Viswanathan, "Whatever This Is, It Isn't Realism," *National Interest*, June 15, 2025, http://nationalinterest.org/feature/whatever-this-is-it-isnt-realism; Samuel Samson, "The Need for Civilizational Allies in Europe," Substack, U.S. State Department, May 27, 2025, http://statedept.substack.com/p/the-need-for-civilizational-allies-in-europe; and Joseph Winter, "Trump Tells Military to Prepare for 'Action' Against Islamist Militants in Nigeria," BBC News, November 3, 2025, http://bbc.com/news/articles/cev18jy21w7o.

123. For instance, in August 2025 Trump imposed 50 percent tariffs on India, despite India being a critical ally in the coalition against China. See Ali Abbas Ahmadi, Soutik Biswas, and Archana Shukla, "Trump Orders India Tariff Hike to 50% for Buying Russian Oil," BBC News, August 6, 2025, http://bbc.com/news/articles/c1dxr1g4y7yo; Gordon G. Chang, "China Is the Big Winner of the Trump-Putin Summit," *Newsweek*, August 20, 2025, http://newsweek.com/china-big-winner-trump-putin-summit-opinion-2116005; Didi Tang, "Senate Democrats Say Trump's Policies Are Hurting America's Ability to Compete With China," Associated Press, July 14, 2025, http://apnews.com/article/china-trump-usaid-influence-visa-48bb3a3cdb11f8f9622addb3954ff3b9; Paul McLeary, "Hegseth Warns Asia Allies That China Threat is 'Imminent,'" *Politico*, May 30, 2025, http://politico.com/news/2025/05/30/hegseth-warns-asia-allies-that-china-threat-is-imminent-00378700; and Farnoush Amiri, Matthew Lee, and Didi Tang, "Marco Rubio Warns China is America's 'Biggest Threat,' Affirms Value of NATO Alliance," Associated Press, January 15, 2025, http://apnews.com/article/marco-rubio-trump-secretary-state-senate-nomination-7ad1ad16ed95a213706c18b613b630b5.

124. Tim Kelly, John Geddie, Ju-min Park, Joyce Lee, Josh Smith, and David Lague, "Trump Shock Spurs Japan to Think About the Unthinkable: Nuclear Arms," Reuters, August 19, 2025, Last Updated August 22, 2025, http://reuters.com/investigations/trump-shock-spurs-japan-think-about-unthinkable-nuclear-arms-2025-08-20; Choe Sang-Hun, "Doubting America's 'Nuclear Umbrella,' Some South Koreans Want Their Own," *New York Times*, August 17, 2024, http://nytimes.com/2024/08/17/world/asia/south-korea-nuclear-arsenal.html; and Ross Andersen, "The Nuclear Club Might Soon Double," *The Atlantic*, July 8, 2025, http://theatlantic.com/magazine/archive/2025/08/nuclear-proliferation-arms-race/683251.

125. Editorial Board, "What America Stands to Lose in the Trade War," *Washington Post*, April 12, 2025, http://washingtonpost.com/opinions/2025/04/12/trump-trade-war-american-power; and Harold James and Marie-Louise James, "How Nostalgia Ruins

Economies," *Foreign Affairs*, May 28, 2025, http://foreignaffairs.com/united-states/how-nostalgia-ruins-economies-trump.

126. Hanna Duggal and Marium Ali, "How Much Will Trump's New Tariffs Hurt Other Countries and U.S. Consumers?" Al Jazeera, April 4, 2025, http://aljazeera.com/news/2025/4/4/how-much-will-trumps-new-tariffs-hurt-other-countries-and-us-consumers; Solcyré Burga, "How Trump's Tariffs Will Impact U.S. Consumers," *Time*, April 1, 2025, http://time.com/7273506/trump-tariffs-us-consumer-impact; Kamal Munir, "Sorry, America, Tariffs Won't Bring Jobs Back," Al Jazeera, April 11, 2025, http://aljazeera.com/opinions/2025/4/11/sorry-america-tariffs-wont-bring-jobs-back; Fareed Zakaria, "Trump's War on Harvard Is Bizarre—and Incredibly Damaging," *Washington Post*, May 30, 2025, http://washingtonpost.com/opinions/2025/05/30/harvard-trump-competition-china-science; Jacob Heilbrunn, "The American Economy Is Paying for Trump's Tariffs," *National Interest*, July 29, 2025, http://nationalinterest.org/feature/the-american-economy-is-paying-for-trumps-tariffs; and Olesya Dmitracova, "Here's How Trump's Tariffs Could Affect Americans," CNN, July 9, 2025, http://cnn.com/2025/07/09/economy/why-tariffs-backfire-trump-intl.

127. "How Golden Ages Really Start—and End," *The Economist*, May 1, 2025, http://economist.com/culture/2025/05/01/how-golden-ages-really-start-and-end.

128. Steven J. Davis quoted in "Hoover Daily Report: Thursday, October 9, 2025," Hoover Institution, October 9, 2025, http://hoover.org/publications/hoover-daily-report/thursday-october-9-2025.

129. The FY26 defense spending request is $848.3 billion, a real dollar cut of $25.4 billion from the year before. Trump did add $150 billion in reconciliation funds for defense in his Big Beautiful Bill Act, however the vast majority of these additional dollars will be spent in FY2026 and this does not increase the baseline defense budget for long-term competition with China and Russia (David A. Deptula, "President Trump Decreased U.S. Defense Budgets, Here's The Real Impact," *Forbes*, July 16, 2025, http://forbes.com/sites/davedeptula/2025/07/16/why-president-donald-trump-might-increase-americas-defense-budget; Editorial Board, "Trump Isn't Rebuilding the U.S. Military," *Wall Street Journal*, July 11, 2025, http://wsj.com/opinion/trump-isnt-rebuilding-the-u-s-military-national-security-defense-spending-266b41e6; "Committee Releases FY26 Defense Bill," Press Release, United States House Committee on Appropriations, June 9, 2025, http://appropriations.house.gov/news/press-releases/committee-releases-fy26-defense-bill; Joe Gould, Connor O'Brien, Eric Bazail-Eimil, and Robbie Gramer, "Making Sense of Trump's Defense Spending Math," *Politico*, May 5, 2025, http://politico.com/newsletters/national-security-daily/2025/05/05/making-sense-of-trumps-defense-spending-math-00329045; and "The White House Office of Management and Budget Releases the President's Fiscal Year 2026 Skinny Budget," Briefings & Statements, Trump White House, May 2, 2025, http://whitehouse.gov/briefings-statements/2025/05/the-white-house-office-of-management-and-budget-releases-the-presidents-fiscal-year-2026-skinny-budget).

130. "In Riyadh, President Trump Charts the Course for a Prosperous Future in the Middle East," May 13, 2025, Articles, Trump White House, http://whitehouse.gov/articles/2025/05/in-riyadh-president-trump-charts-the-course-for-a-prosperous-future-in-the-middle-east.

131. "GDP Update," U.S. Congress Joint Economic Committee, Q2 2025, July 30, 2025.

132. World Bank Open Data, "GDP per Capita (current US$)—China, United States," World Bank, Accessed July 16, 2025, http://data.worldbank.org/indicator/NY.GDP.PCAP.CD?locations=CN-US.

133. World Bank Open Data, "GDP (current US$)—United States, World, China," World Bank, Accessed July 16, 2025, http://data.worldbank.org/indicator/NY.GDP.MKTP.CD?locations=US-1W-CN.

134. "The American Economy Has Left Other Rich Countries in the Dust," *The Economist*, October 14, 2024, http://economist.com/special-report/2024/10/14/the-american-economy-has-left-other-rich-countries-in-the-dust.

135. International Monetary Fund Data, "Currency Composition of Official Foreign Exchange Reserves (COFER)," International Monetary Fund, Accessed August 11, 2025, http://data.imf.org/en/Data-Explorer?datasetUrn=IMF.STA:COFER(7.0.0).

136. "American Productivity Still Leads the World," *The Economist*, October 14, 2024, http://economist.com/special-report/2024/10/14/american-productivity-still-leads-the-world.

137. Colin Grabow, "The United States Remains a Manufacturing Powerhouse," *Cato at Liberty*, Cato Institute, October 25, 2023, http://cato.org/blog/united-states-remains-manufacturing-powerhouse; and "U.S. Manufacturing Economy," Applied Economics Office, National Institute of Standards and Technology, Last Updated November 15, 2024, http://nist.gov/el/applied-economics-office/manufacturing/manufacturing-economy/total-us-manufacturing.

138. "Discovery: R&D Activity and Research Publications," National Science Board, July 23, 2025, http://ncses.nsf.gov/pubs/nsb20257.

139. Xinmei Shen, "China's AI Capital Spending Set to Reach Up to US$98 Billion in 2025 Amid Rivalry With U.S.," *South China Morning Post*, June 25, 2025, http://scmp.com/tech/tech-war/article/3315805/chinas-ai-capital-spending-set-reach-us98-billion-2025-amid-rivalry-us; and Saritha Rai and Seth Fiegerman, "The AI Showdown: How the U.S. and China Stack Up," Bloomberg, August 6, 2025, http://bloomberg.com/news/articles/2025-08-06/who-is-winning-the-artificial-intelligence-race-the-us-or-china.

140. Saritha Rai and Seth Fiegerman, "The AI Showdown: How the U.S. and China Stack Up," Bloomberg, August 6, 2025, http://bloomberg.com/news/articles/2025-08-06/who-is-winning-the-artificial-intelligence-race-the-us-or-china; and Danielle Popov, "U.S. Underestimating China's AI Progress, OpenAI's Sam Altman Says," *South China Morning Post*, August 19, 2025, http://scmp.com/tech/tech-war/article/3322364/us-underestimating-chinas-ai-progress-openais-sam-altman-says.

141. Long Phan et al., "Humanity's Last Exam," 2025, Accessed August 24, 2025, http://agi.safe.ai.

142. Konstantin F. Pilz, Robi Rahman, James Sanders, and Lennart Heim, "Trends In AI Supercomputers," Epoch AI, April 23, 2025, Accessed August 22, 2025, http://epoch.ai/blog/trends-in-ai-supercomputers.

143. "Research and Development," chapter in "The 2025 AI Index Report," Nestor Maslej et al., AI Index Steering Committee, Institute for Human-Centered AI, Stanford University, April 2025, http://hai.stanford.edu/assets/files/hai_ai-index-report-2025_chapter1_final.pdf.

144. Chenggang Zhao et al., "Insights Into DeepSeek-V3: Scaling Challenges and Reflections on Hardware for AI Architectures," *Proceedings of the 52nd Annual International Symposium on Computer Architecture* (2025): 1731-1745.

145. "U.S. Energy Facts Explained," U.S. Energy Information Administration, Last Updated July 15, 2024, Accessed August 11, 2025, http://eia.gov/energyexplained/us-energy-facts/imports-and-exports.php; "The United States Exported 30% of the Energy It Produced in 2024," In-Brief Analysis, U.S. Energy Information Administration, August 12, 2025, http://eia.gov/todayinenergy/detail.php?id=65924#; and "Energy-Related Products," Trade Shifts, 2024, United States International Trade Commission, http://usitc.gov/research_and_analysis/tradeshifts/2024/energy.

146. Gavin Maguire, "Key U.S. Natural Gas Trends to Track as LNG Exports Hit New Highs," Reuters, August 14, 2025, http://reuters.com/markets/commodities/key-us-natural-gas-trends-track-lng-exports-hit-new-highs-2025-08-14.

147. "World University Rankings 2025," *Times Higher Education*, http://timeshighereducation.com/world-university-rankings/latest/world-ranking.

148. Stuart Anderson, "Immigrant Nobel Prize Winners Continue to Impress," *Forbes*, October 5, 2023, http://forbes.com/sites/stuartanderson/2023/10/05/immigrant-nobel-prize-winners-continue-to-impress.

149. "Clarivate Reveals Highly Cited Researchers 2024 List," Clarivate, November 19, 2024, http://clarivate.com/news/clarivate-reveals-highly-cited-researchers-2024-list.

150. Aaron Mehta and Valerie Insinna, "$895.2 Billion Compromise NDAA Released, Sliding Under Fiscal Responsibility Act Cap Levels," *Breaking Defense*, December 7, 2024, http://breakingdefense.com/2024/12/895-2-billion-compromise-ndaa-released-sliding-under-fiscal-responsibility-act-cap-levels.

151. "Unprecedented Rise in Global Military Expenditure as European and Middle East Spending Surges," Press Release, Stockholm International Peace Research Institute, April 28, 2025, http://sipri.org/media/press-release/2025/unprecedented-rise-global-military-expenditure-european-and-middle-east-spending-surges; and "The United States Spends More on Defense Than the Next 9 Countries Combined," Defense Spending, Peter G. Peterson, Foundation, Last Updated May 5, 2025, http://pgpf.org/article/the-united-states-spends-more-on-defense-than-the-next-9-countries-combined.

152. Jon Harper, "Congress Sets Pentagon Research, Development, Test and Evaluation Spending at $141B," DefenseScoop, March 17, 2025, http://defensescoop.com/2025/03/17/congress-defense-appropriations-2025-rdte-spending-141b; and "Russia to Hike Defense Spending by a Quarter in 2025," Al Jazeera, September 30, 2024, http://aljazeera.com/news/2024/9/30/russia-to-hike-defence-spending-by-a-quarter-in-2025.

153. "Ukraine the World's Biggest Arms Importer; United States' Dominance of Global Arms Exports Grows as Russian Exports Continue to Fall," Press Release, Stockholm International Peace Research Institute, Accessed August 5, 2025, http://sipri.org/media/press-release/2025/ukraine-worlds-biggest-arms-importer-united-states-dominance-global-arms-exports-grows-russian; and SIPRI Arms Industry Database, "The SIPRI Top 100 Arms-Producing and Military Services Companies in the World, 2023," Stockholm International Peace Research Institute, Accessed August 5, 2025, http://sipri.org/visualizations/2024/sipri-top-100-arms-producing-and-military-services-companies-world-2023.

154. "Importance of the Nuclear Triad," U.S. Department of Defense, Accessed August 11, 2025, http://defense.gov/Multimedia/Experience/Americas-Nuclear-Triad; and "Federation of American Scientists Releases Latest United States Edition of Nuclear Notebook," Federation of American Scientists, January 13, 2025, http://fas.org/publication/united-states-edition-of-nuclear-notebook-2025.

155. Global Firepower Index, "2025 United States Military Strength," Global Firepower, Accessed August 5, 2025, http://globalfirepower.com/country-military-strength-detail.php?country_id=united-states-of-america; and Global Firepower Index, "Armored Fighting Vehicle Strength by Country (2025)," Global Firepower, Accessed August 12, 2025, http://globalfirepower.com/armor-apc-total.php.

156. Global Firepower Index, "Military Aircraft Fleet Strength by Country (2025)," Global Firepower, Accessed August 12, 2025, http://globalfirepower.com/aircraft-total.php.

157. "Zumwalt," *All Hands Magazine of the U.S. Navy*, http://allhands.navy.mil/Features/Zumwalt; Global Firepower Index, "Navy Fleet by Tonnage by Country (2025)," Global Firepower, Accessed August 13, 2025, http://globalfirepower.com/navy-force-by-tonnage.php; Global Firepower Index, "Navy Fleet Strength by Country (2025)," Global Firepower, Accessed August 13, 2025, http://globalfirepower.com/navy-ships.php; Global Firepower Index, "Aircraft Carrier Fleet Strength by Country (2025)," Global Firepower, Accessed August 13, 2025, http://globalfirepower.com/navy-aircraft-carriers.php; and "Submarine Force Facts," Commander, Submarine Force Atlantic, http://sublant.usff.navy.mil/About-Us/Submarine-Facts.

158. Mohammed Hussein and Mohammed Haddad, "Infographic: U.S. Military Presence Around the World," Al Jazeera, September 10, 2021, http://aljazeera.com/news/2021/9/10/infographic-us-military-presence-around-the-world-interactive; "Military Satellites by Country 2025," World Population Review, Accessed August 5, 2025, http://worldpopulationreview.com/country-rankings/military-satellite-by-country; "UCS Satellite Database," Union of Concerned Scientists, Accessed August 25, 2025, http://ucs.org/resources/satellite-database; and Robert Switzer and Catherine A. Theohary, "Defense Primer: U.S. Cyber Command (USCYBERCOM)," Congress.gov, June 25, 2025, http://congress.gov/crs-product/IF13042.

159. Office of the Director of National Intelligence, *Annual Threat Assessment of the U.S. Intelligence Community* (Washington, DC: Office of the Director of National Intelligence, 2025), http://dni.gov/files/ODNI/documents/assessments/ATA-2025-Unclassified-Report.pdf.

160. Lizette Chapman et al., "Silicon Valley Is Coming for the Pentagon's $1 Trillion Budget," *Bloomberg*, May 8, 2025, http://bloomberg.com/graphics/2025-silicon-valley-targets-pentagon-budget; and Mike Stone, "U.S. 'Replicator' Drone Program to Cost $500 Million per Year, Pentagon Says," Reuters, March 11, 2024, http://reuters.com/world/us/us-replicator-drone-program-cost-500-million-per-year-pentagon-says-2024-03-11.

161. Jinghan Zeng, "The U.S. Factor in Chinese Perceptions of Militarized Artificial Intelligence," *International Affairs* 101, no. 2 (March 2025): http://doi.org/10.1093/ia/iiae323.

162. Michael Drummond, "Is a Ceasefire in Ukraine Finally on the Table? Here's What We Know—as Fighting Grinds On," Sky News, August 7, 2025, http://news.sky.com/story/is-a-ceasefire-in-ukraine-finally-on-the-table-heres-what-we-know-as-fighting-grinds-on-13408008; "Trump's 20-Point Gaza Peace Plan in Full," BBC News, October 9, 2025,

http://bbc.com/news/articles/c70155nked7o; Paulin Kola, "Hundreds of Israeli Ex-Officials Appeal to Trump to Help End Gaza War," BBC News, August 4, 2025, http://bbc.com/news/articles/crkznje8nz8o; Scott Detrow and Diaa Hadid, "President Trump Says the U.S. Helped Broker Ceasefire Between India and Pakistan," NPR, May 10, 2025, http://npr.org/2025/05/10/nx-s1-5394453/president-trump-says-the-us-helped-broker-ceasefire-between-india-and-pakistan; Associated Press, "Congo and Rwanda Sign a U.S.-Mediated Peace Deal Aimed at Ending Decades of Bloody Conflict," NBC News, June 28, 2025, http://nbcnews.com/world/africa/congo-rwanda-sign-us-mediated-peace-deal-aimed-ending-decades-bloody-c-rcna215702; John Reed and Sun Narin, "Thailand and Cambodia Set for Ceasefire Talks After Donald Trump Trade Threat," *Financial Times*, July 26, 2025, http://ft.com/content/49daa1b2-3d0e-4fdf-a0fd-c747883ee4be; Hannah Ellis-Petersen, "Uneasy India-Pakistan Ceasefire Holds but Is a Return to War Inevitable?," *The Guardian*, May 20, 2025, http://theguardian.com/world/2025/may/20/uneasy-india-pakistan-ceasefire-holds-but-is-a-return-to-war-inevitable; and Steve Daines, "A Peace Deal for Armenia and Azerbaijan," *Wall Street Journal*, July 29, 2025, http://wsj.com/opinion/a-peace-deal-for-armenia-and-azerbaijan-99373485.

163.   Quint Forgey, "'The Dawn of a New Middle East': Trump Celebrates Abraham Accords With White House Signing Ceremony," *Politico*, September 15, 2020, http://politico.com/news/2020/09/15/trump-abraham-accords-palestinians-peace-deal-415083; Alexandre Kateb, "The Abraham Accords After Gaza: A Change of Context," Carnegie Endowment for International Peace, April 25, 2025, http://carnegieendowment.org/research/2025/04/the-abraham-accords-after-gaza-a-change-of-context?lang=en; "UAE to Invest $1.4 Trillion in U.S. Over 10 Years, Says Sheikh Mohamed in Show of Strong Trump-era Ties," *Economic Times*, May 15, 2025, http://economictimes.indiatimes.com/news/international/global-trends/uae-to-invest-1-4-trillion-in-us-over-10-years-says-sheikh-mohamed-in-show-of-strong-trump-era-ties/articleshow/121194922.cms?from=mdr; "Qatar's QIA Plans to at Least Double Annual U.S. Investments Over Next Decade," Reuters, May 20, 2025, http://reuters.com/world/middle-east/qatars-qia-plans-least-double-annual-us-investments-over-next-decade-2025-05-20; Aaron Y. Zelin, "Trump Meets Sharaa: Writing a New Chapter in U.S.-Syria Relations," Policy Analysis, Washington Institute for Near East Policy, May 14, 2025, http://washingtoninstitute.org/policy-analysis/trump-meets-sharaa-writing-new-chapter-us-syria-relations; "Turkey's Strongman Is Becoming Donald Trump's Point Man," *The Economist*, July 3, 2025, http://economist.com/europe/2025/07/03/turkeys-strongman-is-becoming-donald-trumps-point-man; Adam Weinstein and Steven Simon, "The Fading of Old Irritants: U.S.–Türkiye Relations in a Post–Assad Landscape," Quincy Institute for Responsible Statecraft, August 12, 2025, http://quincyinst.org/research/the-fading-of-old-irritants-u-s-turkiye-relations-in-a-post-assad-landscape; and "U.S. Relations With Iran: 1953–2025," Council on Foreign Relations, Accessed August 12, 2025, http://cfr.org/timeline/us-relations-iran-1953-2025.

164.   Wenran Jiang, "Why U.S. Allies Are Resisting China's Charm Offensive on Trade," *South China Morning Post*, August 24, 2025, http://scmp.com/opinion/china-opinion/article/3322705/why-us-allies-are-resisting-chinas-charm-offensive-trade.

165.   "Lowy Institute Asia Power Index 2024 Edition," Lowy Institute, Accessed August 6, 2025, http://power.lowyinstitute.org.

166.   G. John Ikenberry, *Liberal Leviathan: The Origins, Crisis, and Transformation of the American World Order* (Princeton, NJ: Princeton University Press, 2011); and Kori Schake,

"A Tale of Two Hegemons: The Anglo-American Roots of the Postwar International System," War on the Rocks, December 21, 2017, http://warontherocks.com/2017/12/a-tale-of-two-hegemons-the-anglo-american-roots-of-the-postwar-international-system.

167. Daniel H. Rosen et al., "After the Fall: China's Economy in 2025," Rhodium Group, December 31, 2024, http://rhg.com/research/after-the-fall-chinas-economy-in-2025; Jason Douglas, "China's Economic Growth Fell to Near-Historic Lows as Covid Took a Bite," *Wall Street Journal*, January 17, 2023, http://wsj.com/articles/chinas-economic-growth-fell-to-near-historic-lows-as-covid-took-a-bite-11673921199.

168. Michael Pettis, "The Relationship Between Chinese Debt and China's Trade Surplus," Carnegie Endowment For International Peace, February 6, 2025, http://carnegieendowment.org/posts/2025/02/the-relationship-between-chinese-debt-and-chinas-trade-surplus?lang=en; "China Debt Problem," Reuters Graphics, Reuters, http://fingfx.thomsonreuters.com/gfx/rngs/CHINA-DEBT-HOUSEHOLD/010030H712Q/index.html; Michael Pettis, "How China Trapped Itself," *Foreign Affairs*, October 5, 2022, http://foreignaffairs.com/china/how-china-trapped-itself; and Logan Wright, "China's Slow-Motion Financial Crisis Is Unfolding as Expected," Center for Strategic and International Studies, September 21, 2022, http://csis.org/analysis/chinas-slow-motion-financial-crisis-unfolding-expected.

169. Xinyi Wu, "China's Youth Jobless Rate Falls Slightly but Remains High After Record Graduation Season," *South China Morning Post*, October 22, 2025, http://scmp.com/economy/article/3329629/chinas-youth-jobless-rate-falls-slightly-remains-high-after-record-graduation-season; and Zen Soo, "China Starts Publishing Youth Jobless Data Again, With a New Method and a Lower Number," Associated Press, January 17, 2024, http://apnews.com/article/china-youth-unemployment-slowdown-321cd96377ee066915fc39232b9477c3.

170. Laura Bicker, "China's Ageing Population: A Demographic Crisis Is Unfolding for Xi," BBC News, April 2, 2024, http://bbc.com/news/world-asia-china-68595450; George F. Will, "Why China Will Become Ever More Dangerous as Its Baby Bust Worsens," *Washington Post*, August 19, 2022, http://washingtonpost.com/opinions/2022/08/19/dangerous-china-demographic-decline; Howard W. French, "A Shrinking China Can't Overtake America," *Foreign Policy*, July 29, 2022, http://foreignpolicy.com/2022/07/29/china-population-decline-demographics-ecomomic-growth; Hal Brands, "The Dangers of China's Decline," *Foreign Policy*, April 14, 2022, http://foreignpolicy.com/2022/04/14/china-decline-dangers; and Andrew S. Erickson and Gabriel B. Collins, "A Dangerous Decade of Chinese Power Is Here," *Foreign Policy*, October 18, 2021, http://foreignpolicy.com/2021/10/18/china-danger-military-missile-taiwan.

171. Micah McCartney, "China's Plan to Tackle Birth Rate Crisis," *Newsweek*, March 9, 2025, http://newsweek.com/china-plan-tackle-birth-rate-population-crisis-2041107.

172. 2024 United Nations, DESA, Population Division. Licensed under Creative Commons license CC BY 3.0 IGO. United Nations, DESA, Population Division. *World Population Prospects 2024*. http://population.un.org/wpp.

173. Sebastian Mallaby, "Demographics Are Destiny," in "What Just Happened: Storm Clouds Loom for China's Economy," *Washington Post*, August 18, 2023, http://washingtonpost.com/opinions/2023/08/18/china-economy-deflation-debt-analysis.

174. Alexandra Stevenson and Zixu Wang, "China's Population Falls, Heralding a Demographic Crisis," *New York Times*, January 17, 2023, http://nytimes.com/2023/01/16/business/china-birth-rate.html.

175. Jonathan A. Czin and John Culver, "Why Xi Still Doesn't Have the Military He Wants," *Foreign Affairs*, August 18, 2025, http://foreignaffairs.com/china/why-xi-still-doesnt-have-military-he-wants; Chris Buckley, "Xi Looks to Tighten Grip After Scandals Shake China's Military Elite," *New York Times*, August 10, 2025, http://nytimes.com/2025/08/10/world/asia/china-military-corruption.html; and "Something Is Amiss in China's Foreign Affairs Leadership," *The Economist*, August 28, 2025, http://economist.com/china/2025/08/28/something-is-amiss-in-chinas-foreign-affairs-leadership.

176. Timothy R. Heath, *The Chinese Military's Doubtful Combat Readiness* (Santa Monica, CA: RAND Corporation, 2025), http://rand.org/pubs/perspectives/PEA830-1.html; M. Taylor Fravel, "Is China's Military Ready For War?," *Foreign Affairs*, July 18, 2025, http://foreignaffairs.com/china/chinas-military-ready-war-xi-jinping-taylor-fravel; Liu Zhen, "U.S. Report Finds Big Weaknesses in China's Defense Industry Base," *South China Morning Post*, February 19, 2022, http://scmp.com/news/china/military/article/3167693/us-report-finds-big-weaknesses-chinas-defence-industry-base; and Steve Sacks, "China's Military Has a Hidden Weakness," *The Diplomat*, April 20, 2021, http://thediplomat.com/2021/04/chinas-military-has-a-hidden-weakness.

177. Kathrin Hille and Edward White, "'Absolute Loyalty': Xi Jinping Turns Anti-Corruption Focus to China's Military," *Financial Times*, July 30, 2023, http://ft.com/content/279a90a3-c550-40a2-9484-8a6eebca628b.

178. Chris Buckley, "Senior Chinese General Is Ousted on Corruption Charges," *New York Times*, October 17, 2025, http://nytimes.com/2025/10/17/world/asia/china-military-general-he-corruption.html.

179. Ibid.

180. David Pierson, "Xi's Military Purges Show Unease About China's Nuclear Forces," *New York Times*, November 12, 2025, http://nytimes.com/2025/11/12/world/asia/xi-trump-military-purges.html; M. Taylor Fravel, "Is China's Military Ready For War?," *Foreign Affairs*, July 18, 2025, http://foreignaffairs.com/china/chinas-military-ready-war-xi-jinping-taylor-fravel; and Timothy R. Heath, *The Chinese Military's Doubtful Combat Readiness* (Santa Monica, CA: RAND Corporation, 2025), http://rand.org/pubs/perspectives/PEA830-1.html.

181. Peter Martin and Jennifer Jacobs, "U.S. Intelligence Shows Flawed China Missiles Led Xi to Purge Army," Bloomberg, January 6, 2024, http://bloomberg.com/news/articles/2024-01-06/us-intelligence-shows-flawed-china-missiles-led-xi-jinping-to-purge-military.

182. "China v America: How Xi Jinping Plans to Narrow the Military Gap," *The Economist*, May 8, 2023, http://economist.com/china/2023/05/08/china-v-america-how-xi-jinping-plans-to-narrow-the-military-gap.

183. Ashley J. Tellis et al., *Measuring National Power in the Postindustrial Age* (Santa Monica, CA: RAND Corporation, 2000), http://rand.org/content/dam/rand/pubs/monograph_reports/MR1110/RAND_MR1110.pdf.

184. Robert E. Baldwin and Anne O. Krueger, eds., *The Structure and Evolution of Recent U.S. Trade Policy* (Chicago: University of Chicago Press, 1984), 5-31.

185. Benn Steil, *The Marshall Plan: Dawn of the Cold War* (New York: Simon & Schuster, 2018).

186. Ashley J. Tellis, "Interdependence Imperiled? Economic Decoupling in an Era of Strategic Competition" in *Strategic Asia: Reshaping Economic Interdependence in the Indo-Pacific*, Ashley J. Tellis and Michael Wills eds. (Seattle, WA: National Bureau of Asian Research, 2023), http://nbr.org/publication/interdependence-imperiled-economic-decoupling-in-an-era-of-strategic-competition.

187. U.S. International Trade Commission, *The Economic Effects of Significant U.S. Import Restraints*, Ninth Update 2017, Washington, DC: U.S. International Trade Commission, September 2017, http://usitc.gov/publications/332/pub4726.pdf; and Erica York, "Separating Tariff Facts from Tariff Fictions," Cato Institute, April 16, 2024, http://cato.org/publications/separating-tariff-facts-tariff-fictions.

188. World Bank Open Data, "Final Consumption Expenditure (current US$)—United States, China, European Union," World Bank, Accessed July 16, 2025, http://data.worldbank.org/indicator/NE.CON.TOTL.CD?contextual=max&locations=US-CN-EU; and Gina Chon and Pete Sweeney, "Global Economy Can Thank U.S. Consumers," Reuters, August 31, 2022, http://reuters.com/breakingviews/global-economy-can-thank-us-consumers-2022-08-30.

189. George Modelski and William R. Thompson, *Leading Sectors and World Powers: The Coevolution of Global Politics and Economics* (Columbia, SC: University of South Carolina Press, 1996).

190. Robert D. Atkinson et al., *Understanding and Comparing National Innovation Systems: The U.S., Korea, China, Japan, and Taiwan* (Washington, DC: Information Technology and Innovation Foundation, 2025).

191. "American Productivity Still Leads the World," *The Economist*, October 14, 2024, http://economist.com/special-report/2024/10/14/american-productivity-still-leads-the-world.

192. David H. Autor, David Dorn, and Gordon H. Hanson, "The China Shock: Learning From Labor Market Adjustment to Large Changes in Trade," Working Paper, National Bureau of Economic Research, January 2016, http://nber.org/papers/w21906.

193. Daniel Bell, *The Coming of Post-Industrial Society: A Venture in Social Forecasting* (New York: Basic Books, 1973), 20.

194. Ashley J. Tellis, "A Tempestuous Hegemon in a Tumultuous Era" in *Strategic Asia 2021–2022: Navigating Tumultuous Times*, Ashley J. Tellis, Alison Szalwinski, and Michael Wills eds. (Seattle, WA: National Bureau of Asian Research, 2022).

195. Zachary Basu, "'The Greatest Thing Ever Invented': Tariffs Become Trump's Miracle Cure," Axios, September 25, 2024, http://axios.com/2024/09/25/trump-tariffs-economic-policies-harris; Robert Zoellick, "An Economic Agenda for the Class of 2028," *Wall Street Journal*, July 20, 2025, http://wsj.com/opinion/an-economic-agenda-for-the-class-of-2028-debt-prices-spending-trade-bb37f936; Tara Watson and Jonathon Zars, "100 Days of Immigration Under the Second Trump Administration," Brookings Institution, April 29, 2025, http://brookings.edu/articles/100-days-of-immigration-under-the-second-trump-administration; John Kruzel, "With Sweeping Actions, Trump Tests U.S. Constitutional Order," Reuters, March 21, 2025, http://reuters.com/world/us/with-sweeping-actions-trump-tests-us-constitutional-order-2025-03-21; Catherine Rampell, "Trump Is Killing One of Our Strongest Exports," *Washington Post*, April 15, 2025, http://washingtonpost.com/opinions/2025/04/15/trump-higher-education-colleges-trade-

war; and A. Martínez and Destinee Adams, "Trump's Harvard Funding Cuts Don't Put 'America First,' Says Massachusetts Governor," NPR, April 29, 2025, http://npr.org/2025/04/29/nx-s1-5380237/trump-harvard-funding-cuts-impact-economy.

196. Michael Dunne, "Why Americans Can't Buy the World's Best Electric Car," *New York Times*, July 8, 2025, http://nytimes.com/2025/07/08/opinion/byd-china-car-ev.html; and Robert D. Atkinson, *China Is Rapidly Becoming a Leading Innovator in Advanced Industries* (Washington, DC: Information Technology and Innovation Foundation, 2024), http://itif.org/publications/2024/09/16/china-is-rapidly-becoming-a-leading-innovator-in-advanced-industries.

197. Ibid.

198. James Dobbins and Ali Wyne, "The U.S. Can't 'Out-China' China," *The Hill*, December 30, 2018, http://thehill.com/opinion/international/423225-the-us-cant-out-china-china.

199. Taylore Roth et al., *Critical Technology Supply Chains in the Asia-Pacific: Options for the United States to De-risk and Diversify* (Seattle, WA: National Bureau of Asian Research, 2023); and Sharon E. Burke et al., *Critical Minerals: Global Supply Chains and Indo-Pacific Geopolitics* (Seattle, WA: National Bureau of Asian Research, 2022), http://nbr.org/publication/critical-minerals-global-supply-chains-and-indo-pacific-geopolitics.

200. Ashley J. Tellis, "The Geopolitics of the TTIP and the TPP," in *Power Shifts and New Blocs in the Global Trading System*, Sanjaya Baru and Suvi Dogra eds. (Abingdon: Routledge, 2015).

201. A cogent defense of what a sensibly restructured approach to international trade might look like can be found in Jennifer Kavanagh and Mariano-Florentino (Tino) Cuéllar, "U.S. Engagement in the Indo-Pacific: Don't Trade Away Trade," Paper, Carnegie Endowment for International Peace, June 25, 2024, http://carnegieendowment.org/research/2024/06/us-engagement-in-the-indo-pacific-dont-trade-away-trade?lang=en.

202. Edward Alden, *Failure to Adjust: How Americans Got Left Behind in the Global Economy* (Lanham, MD: Rowman & Littlefield Publishers, 2016).

203. Robert D. Atkinson, *China Is Rapidly Becoming a Leading Innovator in Advanced Industries* (Washington, DC: Information Technology and Innovation Foundation, 2024), http://itif.org/publications/2024/09/16/china-is-rapidly-becoming-a-leading-innovator-in-advanced-industries.

204. A likely-apocryphal quip from Otto von Bismarck captures the United States' geographic advantages: "The Americans are a very lucky people. They're bordered to the north and south by weak neighbors, and to the east and west by fish."

205. Ashley J. Tellis, "Seeking Alliances and Partnerships: The Long Road to Confederationism in U.S. Grand Strategy," in *Strategic Asia 2014–15: U.S. Alliances and Partnerships at the Center of Global Power*, Ashley J. Tellis, Abraham M. Denmark, and Greg Chaffin eds. (Seattle, WA: National Bureau of Asian Research, 2014), 1–40.

206. Ibid.

207. Edward Lucas, "America Will Miss Europe's Dependence When It's Gone," *Foreign Policy*, April 23, 2025, http://foreignpolicy.com/2025/04/23/us-europe-trump-nato-eu-defense-military-weapons-intelligence-security-russia.

208. Anthony Reuben, "How Much Do Nato Members Spend on Defense?," BBC News, February 18, 2025, http://bbc.com/news/world-44717074.

209. World Bank Open Data, "GDP (current US$)—United States, Japan, Korea, Rep., Australia, Philippines," World Bank, Accessed August 25, 2025, http://data.worldbank.org/indicator/NY.GDP.MKTP.CD?end=2024&locations=US-JP-KR-AU-PH&start=2023.

210. Anna M. Dowd and Stephen J. Flanagan, "Time to Reassess the Costs of Euro-Atlantic Security," RAND Corporation, February 17, 2025, http://rand.org/pubs/commentary/2025/02/time-to-reassess-the-costs-of-euro-atlantic-security.html; and António Costa, "Strengthening EU Defense Won't Undermine the Transatlantic Alliance," *Financial Times*, June 12, 2025, http://ft.com/content/c8cca281-7190-4fbf-a657-eaa79bc93642.

211. King Mallory et al., *Burdensharing and Its Discontents: Understanding and Optimizing Allied Contributions to the Collective Defense* (Santa Monica, CA: RAND Corporation, 2024); and Jason Davidson, "No 'Free-Riding' Here: European Defense Spending Defies U.S. Critics," *New Atlanticist*, Atlantic Council, March 13, 2023, http://atlanticcouncil.org/blogs/new-atlanticist/no-free-riding-here-european-defense-spending-defies-us-critics.

212. Kurt Campbell and Rush Doshi, "America Alone Can't Match China, but With Our Allies, It's No Contest," *New York Times*, September 7, 2025, http://nytimes.com/2025/09/07/opinion/us-trump-china-allies.html; and Seth Cropsey, *Mayday: The Decline of American Naval Supremacy* (New York: Overlook Press, 2014).

213. Walter Russell Mead, "The Return of James Monroe," Hudson Institute, August 6, 2018, http://hudson.org/foreign-policy/the-return-of-james-monroe; and Jay Sexton, "The Many Faces of the Monroe Doctrine," War on the Rocks, December 4, 2023, http://warontherocks.com/2023/12/the-many-faces-of-the-monroe-doctrine.

214. Halford J. Mackinder, "The Geographical Pivot of History," *The Geographical Journal* 23, no. 4 (1904): 421–37, http://jstor.org/stable/1775498; and Nicholas J. Spykman, *America's Strategy in World Politics: The United States and the Balance of Power* (New York: Harcourt, Brace, and Company, 1942).

215. Robert D. Blackwill and Thomas Wright, *The End of World Order and American Foreign Policy* (New York: Council on Foreign Relations, 2020); and Charles Edel and Siddharth Mohandas, "Enhancing Forward Defense: The Role of Allies and Partners in the Indo-Pacific," Center for a New American Security, October 15, 2020, http://cnas.org/publications/commentary/enhancing-forward-defense-the-role-of-allies-and-partners-in-the-indo-pacific.

216. American foreign policy decisions frequently leave allies in the dark. European leaders in preceding decades had first learned from television and the front pages about President John F. Kennedy's 1962 Cuban Missile Crisis, President Lyndon Johnson's 1965 escalation in Vietnam, President Richard Nixon's 1971 unilateral cancellation of the international convertibility of the U.S. dollar to gold, Nixon's 1971 opening to China, Secretary of State Henry Kissinger's 1973–74 diplomacy during the Yom Kippur War, President Ronald Reagan's 1983 Strategic Defense Initiative, President Bill Clinton's 1994 abrupt troop withdrawal from Somalia, and President George W. Bush's 2001 war on terrorism (Blackwill and Fontaine, *Lost Decade*, 106).

217. Doug Bandow et al., "Are America's Alliances a Source of Strength or a Burden as It Competes With China?," Brookings Institution, May 15, 2025, http://brookings.edu/articles/are-americas-alliances-a-source-of-strength-or-a-burden-as-it-competes-with-china; and Mohammed Soliman and Vincent Carchidi, "Re-Balancing the Strategy of

Tech Containment," Analysis, Foreign Policy Research Institute, September 23, 2024, http://fpri.org/article/2024/09/re-balancing-the-strategy-of-tech-containment.

218.   Ashley J. Tellis, "Renewing the American Regime: U.S.–China Competition Beyond Ukraine," Marshall Briefs, CSIS Briefs, The Marshall Papers, Center for Strategic and International Studies, September 12, 2022, http://csis.org/analysis/renewing-american-regime-us-china-competition-beyond-ukraine.

219.   Graham Allison, "Averting the Grandest Collision of All Time," in *Can Asians Think of Peace?*, Kishore Mahbubani, Varigonda Kesava Chandra, and Kristen Tang eds. (Singapore: Springer, 2025), 107-109; and Scott Kennedy, "U.S.-China Relations in 2024: Managing Competition Without Conflict," Center for Strategic and International Studies, January 3, 2024, http://csis.org/analysis/us-china-relations-2024-managing-competition-without-conflict.

220.   Thomas R. Bates, "Gramsci and the Theory of Hegemony," *Journal of the History of Ideas* 36, no. 2 (April-June, 1975): 351-366, http://jstor.org/stable/2708933.

221.   Kenneth Waltz, *Theory of International Politics* (Long Grove, IL: Waveland Press, 2010); and John J. Mearsheimer, *The Tragedy of Great Power Politics* (New York: W.W. Norton and Co., 2001).

222.   See Timothy W. Crawford, "Preventing Enemy Coalitions: How Wedge Strategies Shape Power Politics," *International Security* 35, no. 4 (2011): 155–189; Gadi Heimann, Andreas Kruck. Deganit Paikowsky, and Bernhard Zangl, "Cooptation in Great Power Rivalries: A Conceptual Framework," *Contemporary Security Policy* 46, no. 1 (2025): 8–36; and Andreas Kruck and Bernhard Zangl, "It Pays to Be Generous: How Cooptation Transforms Power Rivalries," *Contemporary Security Policy* 46, no. 1 (2025): 37-65.

223.   David Engerman, "Ideology and the Origins of the Cold War, 1917–1962" chapter in *The Cambridge History of the Cold War*, Melvyn P. Leffler and Odd Arne Westad eds. (Cambridge: Cambridge University Press, 2010), 20–43.

224.   Hal Brands, *American Grand Strategy and the Liberal Order: Continuity, Change, and Options for the Future* (Santa Monica, CA: RAND Corporation, 2016).

225.   Stephen Kotkin, *Armageddon Averted: The Soviet Collapse 1970-2000* (Oxford: Oxford University Press, 2008).

226.   G. John Ikenberry, *Liberal Leviathan: The Origins, Crisis, and Transformation of the American World Order* (Princeton, NJ: Princeton University Press, 2011).

227.   Robert Gilpin, *The Political Economy of International Relations* (Princeton, NJ: Princeton University Press, 1987).

228.   Lara Jakes and Steven Erlanger, "As Trump Demands More Military Spending, NATO Reconsiders What Counts," *New York Times*, May 23, 2025, http://nytimes.com/2025/05/23/world/europe/nato-spending-trump-5-percent.html; Victor Cha, "How Trump Sees Allies and Partners," Analysis, Center for Strategic and International Studies, November 18, 2024, Last Updated January 10, 2025, http://csis.org/analysis/how-trump-sees-allies-and-partners; and Doug Bandow, "Rich and Entitled Allies Don't Need U.S. Support," Cato Institute, March 29, 2021, http://cato.org/commentary/rich-entitled-allies-dont-need-us-support.

229.   Bradley Thayer, "In Defense of Primacy," *National Interest*, no. 86 (November-December 2006).

230. Stephen G. Brooks and William C. Wohlforth, *America Abroad: The United States' Global Role in the 21st Century* (New York: Oxford University Press, 2016).

231. Ibid.

232. G. John Ikenberry, *Liberal Leviathan: The Origins, Crisis, and Transformation of the American World Order* (Princeton, NJ: Princeton University Press, 2011).

233. Eric S. Edelman, *Understanding America's Contested Primacy* (Washington, DC: Center for Strategic and Budgetary Assessments, 2010).

234. Margaret MacMillan, "Making America Alone Again," *Foreign Affairs*, July 21, 2025, http://foreignaffairs.com/united-states/making-america-alone-again-alliances-margaret-macmillan.

235. Evan S. Medeiros and Ashley J. Tellis, "Regime Change Is Not an Option in China—Focus on Beijing's Behavior, Not Its Leadership," *Foreign Affairs*, July 8, 2021, http://foreignaffairs.com/asia/regime-change-not-option-china.

236. The Biden administration instead marked the trigger for military action as when the Iranian leadership directed its scientists to produce a nuclear weapon. See Ellen Knickmeyer, "U.S. Says Iran Moving Forward on a Key Aspect of Developing a Nuclear Bomb," Associated Press, July 19, 2024, http://apnews.com/article/iran-nuclear-weapons-sullivan-blinken-2ba2de90dce5047c4a698b2d57a90e4b.

237. See Dipanjan Roy Chaudhury, "Global Trade at Crossroads: Panel Calls for WTO Reform," *Economic Times*, September 20, 2025, http://economictimes.indiatimes.com/news/economy/foreign-trade/global-trade-at-crossroads-panel-calls-for-wto-reform/articleshow/124013438.cms?from=mdr; Chris Clague, "The Rules-Based Global Trading System Is Mostly Irrelevant," Online Analysis, International Institute for Strategic Studies, April 2, 2025, http://iiss.org/online-analysis/online-analysis/2025/04/the-rules-based-global-trading-system-is-mostly-irrelevant; Michael B.G. Froman, "After The Trade War," *Foreign Affairs*, August 11, 2025, http://foreignaffairs.com/united-states/after-trade-war-michael-froman; Claudia Schmucker and Stormy-Annika Mildner, "What If Multilateral Trade Cooperation Is Dead?," DGAP Memo, German Council on Foreign Relations, no. 3, June 28, 2025, http://dgap.org/en/research/publications/what-if-multilateral-trade-cooperation-dead; "Rumours of the Trade Deal's Death Are Greatly Exaggerated," *The Economist*, June 13, 2024, http://economist.com/finance-and-economics/2024/06/13/rumours-of-the-trade-deals-death-are-greatly-exaggerated; Scott Lincicome, "Checking in on the Death of Globalization™," *Cato at Liberty*, Cato Institute, February 7, 2023, http://cato.org/blog/checking-death-globalizationtm; and Sabine Weyand, "Reports of Globalization's Death Are Greatly Exaggerated," *International Politik Quarterly*, January 4, 2023, http://ip-quarterly.com/en/reports-globalizations-death-are-greatly-exaggerated.

238. "The UK And The Comprehensive and Progressive Agreement for Trans-Pacific Partnership (CPTPP)," Department for Business and Trade and Department for International Trade, Government of the United Kingdom, March 31, 2023, Last Updated August 1, 2025, http://gov.uk/government/collections/the-uk-and-the-comprehensive-and-progressive-agreement-for-trans-pacific-partnershipcptpp.

239. "The Growth of Supply Chain Trade Within the Comprehensive and Progressive Agreement for Trans-Pacific Partnership (CPTPP)," Office of the Chief Economist, Government of Canada, December 2023, http://international.canada.ca/en/global-affairs/corporate/reports/chief-economist/impacts/2023-12-cptpp-growth-supply-chain.

240. "China Fully Prepared to Join CPTPP: Commerce Ministry," State Council of The People's Republic of China, June 19, 2025, http://english.gov.cn/news/202506/19/content_WS6853f2a7c6d0868f4e8f375f.html; Kandy Wong, "What Is The CPTPP and Why Is China Eager To Join?," *South China Morning Post*, May 5, 2022, http://scmp.com/economy/china-economy/article/3176487/what-cptpp-and-why-china-eager-join.

241. World Bank Group, *The African Continental Free Trade Area: Economic and Distributional Effects* (Washington, DC: World Bank, 2020).

242. APEC Policy Support Unit, *Study on Tariffs: Analysis of the RCEP Tariff Liberalization Schedules* (Singapore: Asia-Pacific Economic Cooperation Secretariat, 2022), http://research.apec.org/rcep.

243. Regional Trade Agreements Database, WTO Secretariat, August 21, 2025, http://rtais.wto.org/UI/Charts.aspx.

244. World Bank Group, *Trading for Development in the Age of Global Value Chains* (Washington, DC: International Bank for Reconstruction and Development, 2020).

245. "Global Value and Supply Chains," Policy Issue, OECD, http://oecd.org/en/topics/policy-issues/global-value-and-supply-chains.html; and World Bank Group, *Trading For Development in The Age of Global Value Chains* (Washington, DC: International Bank for Reconstruction and Development, 2020).

246. Meredith Kolsky Lewis, "The Origins of Plurilateralism in International Trade Law," *Journal of World Investment and Trade* 20, no. 5 (2019): 633-653.

247. Jeffrey J. Schott, "The TPP Origins and Outcomes," chapter in *Handbook of International Trade Agreements: Country, Regional and Global Approaches*, Robert E. Looney ed. (Abingdon: Routledge, 2018), 401–11; Peter A. Petri and Michael G. Plummer, "The Economic Effects of the Trans-Pacific Partnership: New Estimates," Peterson Institute for International Economics Working Paper, no. 16-2, East-West Center Workshop on Mega-Regionalism—New Challenges for Trade and Innovation (2016): http://dx.doi.org/10.2139/ssrn.2723413.

248. Alan Wm. Wolff, "Is the World Trade Organization Still Relevant?" Policy Brief 24-15, Peterson Institute for International Economics, December 2024, http://piie.com/publications/policy-briefs/2024/world-trade-organization-still-relevant.

249. I am especially grateful for the insights and policy prescriptions from my exchanges with Robert Zoellick, former U.S. trade representative and World Bank president, who convincingly rejects the contention that the multilateral trading system is dead.

250. World Bank Open Data, "Military Expenditure (% of GDP)—United States," World Bank, Accessed August 11, 2025, http://data.worldbank.org/indicator/MS.MIL.XPND.GD.ZS?end=2023&locations=US&start=2010.

251. Blackwill and Fontaine, *Lost Decade*.

252. Ibid, 160-190.

253. Ibid, 223.

254. John J. Mearsheimer and Stephen M. Walt, "The Case for Offshore Balancing," *Foreign Affairs* 95, no. 4 (2016): 70–83, http://foreignaffairs.com/articles/united-states/2016-06-13/case-offshore-balancing.

255. Hans J. Morgenthau, *Politics Among Nations: The Struggle for Power and Peace* (New York: Alfred A. Knopf, 1948).

256. Robert Gilpin, *The Political Economy of International Relations* (Princeton, NJ: Princeton University Press, 1987).

257. Colin Dueck, *Age of Iron: On Conservative Nationalism* (New York: Oxford University Press, 2020).

258. Stacie E. Goddard, "The Rise and Fall of Great-Power Competition," *Foreign Affairs* 104, no. 3 (May-June 2025), http://foreignaffairs.com/united-states/rise-and-fall-great-power-competition.

259. Paul Kennedy, *The Rise and Fall of the Great Powers: Economic Change and Military Conflict from 1500 to 2000* (New York: Vintage Books, 1987); and Hal Brands, *The Limits of Offshore Balancing* (Carlisle Barracks, PA: United States Army War College Press, 2015).

260. Brands, *The Limits of Offshore Balancing*.

261. Zachary B. Wolf and Curt Merrill, "Trump's 2025 Joint Session Address, Fact Checked and Annotated," CNN, March 5, 2025, http://edition.cnn.com/interactive/2025/03/politics/transcript-speech-trump-congress-annotated-dg.

262. Lara Jakes and Steven Erlanger, "As Trump Demands More Military Spending, NATO Reconsiders What Counts," *New York Times*, May 23, 2025, http://nytimes.com/2025/05/23/world/europe/nato-spending-trump-5-percent.html; Victor Cha, "How Trump Sees Allies and Partners," Analysis, Center for Strategic and International Studies, November 18, 2024, Last Updated January 10, 2025, http://csis.org/analysis/how-trump-sees-allies-and-partners; Doug Bandow, "Rich and Entitled Allies Don't Need U.S. Support," Cato Institute, March 29, 2021, http://cato.org/commentary/rich-entitled-allies-dont-need-us-support; Alex Guillén, "Trump Administration Moves to Repeal Climate 'Holy Grail,'" *Politico*, July 29, 2025, http://politico.com/news/2025/07/29/epa-to-revoke-2009-finding-that-climate-pollution-endangers-humans-00476166; David Gelles, Lisa Friedman, and Brad Plumer, "'Full-On Fight Club': How Trump Is Crushing U.S. Climate Policy," *New York Times*, March 2, 2025, Last Updated August 1, 2025, http://nytimes.com/2025/03/02/climate/trump-us-climate-policy-changes.html; Andrew Jacobs, Saurabh Datar, and Antonio de Luca, "The Evolution of Trump's Views on Foreign Aid," *New York Times*, June 25, 2025, http://nytimes.com/2025/06/25/health/trump-usaid-foreign-aid-video.html; Claire Cranford and Amy Sherman, "Have Trump, Musk and DOGE Really Unearthed 'Fraud' in Government?" Al Jazeera, February 14, 2025, http://aljazeera.com/news/2025/2/14/have-trump-musk-and-doge-really-unearthed-fraud-in-government; and Inu Manak et al., "What Trump Trade Policy Has Achieved Since 'Liberation Day,'" Article, Council on Foreign Relations, July 7, 2025, http://cfr.org/article/what-trump-trade-policy-has-achieved-liberation-day.

263. Michael Beckley, "The Age of American Unilateralism," *Foreign Affairs*, April 16, 2025, http://foreignaffairs.com/united-states/age-american-unilateralism; and Pjotr Sauer and Amy Hawkins, "Xi Jinping Says China Ready to 'Stand Guard Over World Order' on Moscow Visit," *The Guardian*, March 20, 2023, http://theguardian.com/world/2023/mar/20/xi-jinping-vladimir-putin-moscow-ukraine-war.

264. Luke McGee, "Trump May Not Understand How Dangerous the World Is Now," *Foreign Policy*, November 20, 2024, http://foreignpolicy.com/2024/11/20/trump-autocracies-russia-northkorea-ukraine; and Andrea Kendall-Taylor and Richard Fontaine,

"The Axis of Upheaval," *Foreign Affairs*, April 23, 2024, http://foreignaffairs.com/china/axis-upheaval-russia-iran-north-korea-taylor-fontaine.

265. Max Seddon et al., "Donald Trump Fails to Secure Ukraine Deal at Alaska Summit with Vladimir Putin," *Financial Times*, August 15, 2025, Last Updated August 16, 2025, http://ft.com/content/c36899cc-7a15-4f6e-9b7e-531ddaed1dc5.

266. Joseph S. Nye Jr., *The Paradox of American Power: Why the World's Only Superpower Can't Go It Alone* (New York: Oxford University Press, 2002); Mira Rapp-Hooper, *Shields of the Republic: The Triumph and Peril of America's Alliances* (Cambridge, MA: Harvard University Press, 2020); and Malcolm Turnbull, "America's Allies Must Save Themselves," *Foreign Affairs*, June 6, 2025, http://foreignaffairs.com/united-states/americas-allies-must-save-themselves.

267. Ashley J. Tellis, "Uphill Challenges: China's Military Modernization and Asian Security" chapter in *Strategic Asia 2012–2013: Navigating Tumultuous Times*, Ashley J. Tellis and Travis Tanner eds. (Seattle, WA: National Bureau of Asian Research, 2012), 3–24, http://nbr.org/publication/uphill-challenges-chinas-military-modernization-and-asian-security.

268. Richard Haass, *War of Necessity, War of Choice: A Memoir of Two Iraq Wars* (New York: Simon & Schuster, 2009).

269. Trump White House, *National Security Strategy of the United States of America*, November 2025, http://whitehouse.gov/wp-content/uploads/2025/12/2025-National-Security-Strategy.pdf; David E. Sanger, "Superpower Competition: The Missing Chapter in Trump's Security Strategy," *New York Times*, December 7, 2025, http://nytimes.com/2025/12/07/us/politics/trump-security-strategy-superpowers.html; Greg R. Lawson, "The Common-Sense Realism of the National Security Strategy," *National Interest*, December 5, 2025, http://nationalinterest.org/feature/the-common-sense-realism-of-the-national-security-strategy; Jonathan Cheng, "Trump's National-Security Strategy Softens Language on China," *Wall Street Journal*, December 6, 2025, http://wsj.com/world/china/trumps-national-security-strategy-softens-language-on-china-f121ddb3.

270. Secretary of State Madeleine Albright Interview on NBC-TV *The Today Show*, Transcript, February 19, 1998, http://1997-2001.state.gov/statements/1998/980219a.html.

ABOUT THE AUTHOR

Robert D. Blackwill is the Henry A. Kissinger senior fellow for U.S. for-eign policy at the Council on Foreign Relations, a senior fellow at Harvard Kennedy School's Belfer Center for Science and International Affairs, and a distinguished visiting fellow at Stanford University's Hoover Institution. Under President George W. Bush, he was deputy national security advisor for strategic planning, presidential envoy to Iraq, and U.S. ambassador to India from 2001 to 2003. Blackwill was the recipient of the 2007 Bridge-Builder Award for his role in transforming U.S.-India relations, and was honored with India's Padma Bhushan Award in 2016, the first U.S. ambas-sador to India since John Kenneth Galbraith to receive the award.

From 1989 to 1990, he was special assistant to President George H.W. Bush for European and Soviet affairs, and was awarded the Commander's Cross of the Order of Merit by the Federal Republic of Germany for his con-tribution to German unification. Earlier in his career, Blackwill was the U.S. ambassador to conventional arms negotiations with the Warsaw Pact, director for European affairs at the National Security Council, principal deputy assistant secretary of state for political-military affairs, and princi-pal deputy assistant secretary of state for European affairs.

He is the coauthor, with Graham Allison, of *Lee Kuan Yew: The Grand Master's Insights on China, the United States, and the World* (2013) and, with Jennifer M. Harris, of *War by Other Means: Geoeconomics and Statecraft* (2016). Blackwill's new book—*Lost Decade: The US Pivot to Asia and the Rise of Chinese Power*, coauthored with Richard Fontaine of the Center for a New American Secu-rity—was published in 2024. His previous CFR reports include *Revising U.S. Grand Strategy Toward China* (2015, coauthored with Ashley Tellis), *Repair-ing the U.S.-Israel Relationship* (2016, coauthored with Philip H. Gordon), *Containing Russia* (2018, also coauthored with Philip H. Gordon), *Trump's Foreign Policies Are Better Than They Seem* (2019), *The End of World Order and American Foreign Policy* (2020, coauthored with Thomas Wright), *Imple-menting Grand Strategy Toward China: Twenty-Two U.S. Policy Prescriptions* (2020), *The United States, China, and Taiwan: A Strategy to Prevent War* (2021, coauthored with Philip Zelikow), and *No Limits? The China-Russia Relation-ship and U.S. Foreign Policy* (2024, coauthored with Richard Fontaine).